THE STRANGE NEW WORD
OF THE GOSPEL

W Farwell 5/07 40%

The Strange New Word of the Gospel

Re-Evangelizing in the
Postmodern World

Edited by

Carl E. Braaten and Robert W. Jenson

William B. Eerdmans Publishing Company
Grand Rapids, Michigan / Cambridge, U.K.

Wm. B. Eerdmans Publishing Co.
255 Jefferson Ave. S.E., Grand Rapids, Michigan 49503 /
P.O. Box 163, Cambridge CB3 9PU U.K.

Printed in the United States of America

07 06 05 04 03 02   7 6 5 4 3 2 1

Library of Congress Cataloging-in-Publication Data

The strange new word of the Gospel : re-evangelizing in the postmodern world /
edited by Carl E. Braaten and Robert W. Jenson.
    p.   cm.
   Includes bibliographical references.
   Contents: The gospel of affinity / John Milbank — What is a post-Christian? /
Robert W. Jenson — Religion and secularity in a culture of abstraction: on the
integrity of space, time, matter, and motion / David Schindler — Postmodern
irony and Petronian humanism / R. R. Reno — The powerlessness of talking
heads: re-evangelization in a postmodern world, the place of ethics / Philip Turner
— hearts no longer restless: the reawakening of faith in a postmodern West /
Anthony Ugolnik — Truth decay: rethinking evangelism in the new century / Todd
E. Johnson — Orthodoxia, orthopraxis, and seekers / Frank C. Senn — The future
of the apostolic imperative: at the crossroads of world evangelization / Carl E.
Braaten.

   ISBN 0-8028-3947-9 (alk. paper)

   1. Evangelistic work. 2. Postmodernism — Religious aspects — Christianity.
I. Braaten, Carl E., 1929-   II. Jenson, Robert W.
BV3793 .S6775 2002
269′.2 — dc21

                                20002067927

www.eerdmans.com

Contents

Preface

Some years ago advocates of "secular theology" declared that the typical modern is fully secularized, living a contented life without religious purpose or meaning. The secular theologians' appeal to Friedrich Gogarten, Arend T. van Leeuwen, and Dietrich Bonhoeffer was in hindsight a misappropriation of their ideas, but it seemed persuasive at the time. It seemed certain to the secular theologians that the process of secularization, originating in the West, was irresistible and spreading worldwide, and that the church must accommodate the trend and reap its benefits for the gospel. They called for a radical revision of the church's approach to evangelism. In carrying out her mission, they said, the church can no longer presuppose that people are essentially religious or ask religious questions.

The event has been more complicated than predicted. There is indeed massive secularization, but the prophecies of a wholly secular world have not been fulfilled. Instead, religion, if typically of dubious sorts, has made a comeback; we have only to consider the resurgence of fundamentalism in every major religion, and growing preoccupation with magic, mystery, and supernatural forces. Secularists have not disappeared, but they can no longer be regarded as the only typical representatives of the modern mind. The secularist and the superstitious dimensions of modernity co-exist, often in the same person or institution.

Some would call the world that the church is now called to evangelize post-Christian or neopagan. Others call it postmodern, the dominant catchword of those who monitor the trends of the times.

Postmodernism is described as a reaction against the rationalism of the scientific and technocratic world. It reflects the pluralism and relativism of contemporary thought in many fields.

Those who turn to religion are not necessarily finding their way back to church. Most unbelievers in America and other western countries are post-*Christians*. They have been baptized and brought up in a church, but no longer believe and practice the faith. Hence, the need for *re*-evangelization.

Graham Ward begins his editor's introduction to *The Postmodern God: A Theological Reader* with these observations: "Surfing the net is the ultimate postmodern experience. . . . Cyberspace is a cultural metaphor for postmodernism." And he offers this description of the emerging postmodern culture: "a culture of seduction and flagrant, self-consuming sexuality; a culture of increasing sophisticated drugs and drug use; a culture of virtual, video-taped realities." The gospel is a strange word in such culture.

The Christian tradition is a library of theological reflections on the times and situations in which the gospel has been proclaimed. This volume provides a series of theological reflections on the service of the gospel to the emerging postmodern culture of our western world. All but one originated as contributions to theological conferences held at Immanuel Lutheran Church, New York, and Evangelical Lutheran Church of St. Luke, Chicago, in the Fall of 2000, on "The Strange New Word of the Gospel: Re-Evangelizing in the Postmodern World." The essay by Frank C. Senn was presented to a theological conference at St. John's University, Collegeville, Minnesota, on "The Crisis of Christian Worship," in June, 2000.

Carl E. Braaten
Robert W. Jenson

The Gospel of Affinity

JOHN MILBANK

What is postmodernity? Not simply postmodernism as a set of theories, but also postmodernity, as a set of cultural circumstances?

Above all, it means the obliteration of boundaries, the confusion of categories. In the postmodern times in which we live, there is no longer any easy distinction to be made between nature and culture, private interior and public exterior, hierarchial summit and material depth; nor between idea and thing, message and means, production and exchange, product and delivery, the state and the market, humans and animals, humans and machines, image and reality — nor beginning, middle, and end. Everything is made to run into everything else; everything gets blended, undone, and then reblended. There are no longer any clear centers of control, and this means that new weight is given to plurality and the proliferation of difference. However, none of these differences ever assume the status of a distinct essence: rather they are temporary events, destined to vanish and be displaced.

Let us consider some of the main instances of boundary confusion. First of all, the blurring of the distinction between nature and culture. One important aspect of modernity was the sense that human beings could make and remake their own cultural universe. On the other hand, this was usually seen as being done against the backdrop of fixed laws of nature. To some extent, because humans were also recognized as natural, such laws were seen as impinging on the human sphere also — limiting the range of freedom for human self-making. Thus humans were sometimes seen as by nature more fundamentally self-preserving, fear-avoiding, happiness-seeking, sympa-

1

thetic, or else productive creatures. But just recently, all this has appeared to change. First of all, people no longer seem to find any need to identify a human essence — no longer is human auto-creation operating within essential parameters. Humans, it seems, might make anything of themselves. We are our own anarchic laboratory. We can self-manipulate ourselves into a million shapes. Perhaps the only figure of essence that remains here is the idea that humans are productive — but as much the *result* of productive processes, as agents *in command* of production. In consequence, the asymmetrical teleological and hierarchical *aspects* of human existence tend to get flattened out into degrees of intensity along a quantitative scale: no longer are there firm characteristics of childhood, middle or old age; no longer are there clearly any men and women, no longer is there much heterosexuality as opposed to the single, univocal (and therefore transcendentally "homosexual") proliferation of multiple desires.

At the same time, the frontier of culture has so invaded nature that culture appears to be amidst nature, and is no longer like a mind or fortress surmounting it. We can now intervene, technologically, in the organic realm. The prospect of hybridization of pre-given natural kinds has increased exponentially. Here also, boundaries are being transgressed. But already, in the case of the AIDS epidemic and the phenomenon of global warming, the unintended consequences of human intervention involve natural forces becoming much more palpable actors within the cultural sphere. And no doubt genetic manipulation will lead to many more instances of this uncomfortable rebound.

But at a more profound level, our perceptions of nature and culture seem to be merging. Accounts of supposedly "material" realities become more and more ethereal: increasingly, with the decay of any sense that we as humans are governed by natural law, we come to wonder whether "laws" are not a projection by humans upon nature in general. For a long time now, modern physics has tended to think in terms of irreversible temporal processes, engendering not so much laws, as relatively fixed habits. And such habits are not really the habits of material items; it is much more that the material items are the deposits of highly abstract depositions. Likewise, in the sphere of biology, the talk of "codes" and "codings" is not intended in any merely metaphorical sense — if there is metaphor involved here, then it is in the very operation of biological metamorphoses themselves.

Conversely, however, human mental life is increasingly thought of as an embodied life — manipulable in terms of all sorts of narcotic stimuli and regimes of gymnastic exercise. While nature is viewed in terms of the communication of signs, human thought is seen in terms of the processing of electronic impacts in the endlessly complex patternings of plus and minus signs — which point our way through a garden of forking paths, whose only sure fatality is the arrival of the next proximate intersection.

In these circumstances, it is not surprising that, once again, Spinoza enjoys a huge vogue, for he was the philosopher who proclaimed that there is a dual aspect to all phenomena: that the "order and connection of things" is also "the order and connection of ideas." Ideas already inhabit things; but conversely, for us to think is to rearrange reality — not to mirror it, but actively to alter its characteristics.

After the blurring of the boundary between nature and culture comes the new confusion of interior and exterior. And there is a deep connection. For in modern times, the private self guarded the boundary between culture and nature — he went home from public work to the sanctum of his home, with its supposed "natural" family, and looked out upon his cultivated back garden with its intimation of wilderness. Today, however, there is no sanctum. The home, most of all, is invaded by the public voices of the media, with their scarcely veiled instructions and commands. And now, the computer terminal gives domestic access to the global public space — not a real space, but a new, virtual spatiality. Meanwhile, what has happened to the old, real public space — the space for promenading, for civility and overlooked courtship? In the United States, it has already largely vanished. Instead of the public piazza we have the interlocking of semi-private spaces — such that one walks from shopping mall into hotel foyer into a set of office spaces and so forth. Increasingly, houses are situated within enclaves guarded by bad dogs and their unsavory minders. Of course, in this situation, most of our modern "liberal" political discourses start to appear completely meaningless. For they are all predicated on a mutual agreement to protect the right to do what one likes with one's own, so long as this does not interfere with the rights of the other. How can this criterion any longer apply to the real interlocking "rhizome" of material spaces, or to the fluid highway of virtual space? The shared covered walkway is pragmatically negotiated, not constructed according to general formal requirements of universal association, while the telephone and electronic mail give license to endless mutual intrusion and surveillance. "My" website, my informational contribution, has already decided certain things for others, in a space that is theirs as well as mine, like a common grazing ground. No wonder that, for some people, the information highway seems like a simulated communist utopia. This perspective, nevertheless, is deluded, for what is "shared" here is only the immediate proximity of everywhere to everywhere else, which lacks in affinity, or inherited communality — it is therefore only a place without place, a place of total estrangement. The difference from a liberal organization of discrete spaces is really but the self-implosion of a hyper-liberalism: I can choose anything anywhere, but these choices will always be for the choices of others, selecting me. Since anything can now be mine, nothing will really be mine. Liberalism always depended upon the principle that the inalienable private possession is in principle alienable — sellable. But now, everything is entirely possessed as inalienable and already enacted in its constitutive possible alienability all at once.

The new interfolding of inside and outside is exhibited also in a third set of confusions, between all the traditional modern economic categories. It is this confusion that produces the age of *information*. We still find it hard to believe that the production of abstract and ephemeral signs pointing to other signs can have become the driving force of the economy. In the United Kingdom, many still refuse to recognize that the almost total collapse of its automobile industry may actually now give Britain a certain advantage over Germany, where a relatively up-to-date automobile industry still thrives. Backwardness in one phase is an advantage for the next — as Germany, which missed out on the phase of steam, once discovered. In that early industrial era, most people insisted that the production of food must always be the driving economic motor. Instead, as we know, agriculture became subordinated and was itself mechanized. Today, manufacturing is being subordinated and itself informationized. But areas like Los Angeles or London, which work on the most abstract sectors of the economy, are the most booming areas and also the new foci of global command.

In the age of information, production often consists almost immediately (and sometimes entirely so) in the exchange of the product. Likewise, the consumption of the product can already be a type of laboring, while promotion and marketing become themselves the prime generators of profit, rather than its secondary accomplices. And expenditure of informational capital can be equally an investment of such capital in future production. Furthermore, there is no longer any clear disciplinary structure between worker and management operating within a real distinct site, like a factory or an office, nor within a clearly demarcated firm or company. Instead, one has networks of intellectual workers dispersed through real space working somewhat for themselves, and somewhat for varying others. These workers are auto-controlled through the pressures of the need to compete, or the desire for knowledge and influence. No one is telling them how many hours they must labor, but internalized mastery increasingly forces them to work without ceasing. On the other hand, the boundary between this work and their leisure time is becoming hazy, since the seeking out of affective "contacts" is increasingly vital to work performance.

Alongside this sphere of the production of signs, however, it is important to mention also the increased importance of "service" industries — medicine, education, catering, transport, beauticians, etc., etc. — which cater more directly to the needs of minds and bodies. However, these services also are increasingly operated through levels of higher abstraction that allow them to benefit from global expertise and fashion.

In these spheres also, deregulation ensures that hours worked tend to multiply. Meanwhile, in the older manufacturing industries, longer hours are directly enforced, because globalization and informatization have destroyed the bargaining power of manufacturing workers. Thus we can glimpse sight of a gigantic paradox: the increased freedom, deregulation, and differentiation of work in the postmodern era nonetheless permits capital and in particular the multinational corporations to reap vastly increased profit from the vastly increased amount of surplus labor that is now expended in every sphere of production. The times of postmodernity are in no sense post-capitalist times, but rather times of capital writ still larger. Indeed, capital has always been a force of abstraction; today it reaps even larger material benefits from increased abstraction. And even from its inception, capital produced and marketed signs and fashions, and would not have engendered a new abstract equivalence between commodities if it had not done so. In a way, something that has always been latent in modernity is now much more clearly in the foreground.

Perhaps more drastically novel than informatization is a fourth mark of postmodernity: globalization. For this has to do, not with a blurring of divisions within the economic realm, but rather with a merging of this realm with the political sphere. For a long time, the sovereign nation-state assisted the extension and regulation of the free market, but it nonetheless tended to subordinate the making of profit to military strength, and ethnic or national unity. Capitalism always tended to overflow state boundaries, and today it can operate far more effectively by its capacity to shift human, material, and financial resources swiftly, right across the globe. However, this does not mean that the state and politics have come to an end — to the contrary, the market requires, more than ever, the international state-ordering of virtual reality, international legal checks on financial speculations, and international policing of popular or ethnic or religious dissent. Alongside the global market is emerging a kind of global empire — a new sort of postmodern empire, which, as Michael Hardt and Antonio Negri argue, continues the specifically American project of neo-Roman Republican empire.[1] This is not, like the old British and French empires, an empire of center and subordinated colonies, but instead an empire of endlessly expanding frontiers, an empire of inclusion, not remote control, and an empire able to distribute power to its peripheries. But this more invisible, distributed power is all the more a controlling power. Within this empire the United States, the United Nations, various non-governmental agencies, and the multinational corporations all tend to share and blend functions of dominion. The political and the economic are by this means fusing.

So far then, we have seen that postmodernity can be characterized in four ways, all of them having to do with the dissolving of fixed limits. These ways are: (1) the blurring of the nature/culture divide, (2) the merging of public and private, (3) the use of the information economy, and (4) economic and political globalization. But before one asks, how is the church to conduct its mission and articulate its intellectual vision on this postmodern terrain, should we not first ask, does postmodernity, of itself, possess anything like a religious dimension?

Here we should note that the blurring of boundaries has a cultural presupposition. That presupposition is one of *immanence*. An ordering

---

1. See Michael Hardt and Antonio Negri, *Empire* (Cambridge, Mass.: Harvard University Press, 2000). The present essay is heavily indebted to their analyses throughout.

of the world in terms of essences and relative values is linked in some way to teleology and hierarchy, or else, alternatively, to spatialization. In premodernity it was a matter of the former — everything had its appointed goal and relative value in relation to a distant, transcendental source that was equally foundation and finality. Both thought and social nature mirrored this assumption. In modernity, by contrast, from about 1300 onwards, the world was gradually accorded full reality, meaning, and value in itself, without reference to transcendence: what Gilles Deleuze called "the plane of immanence" was born. But in modern times this plane was seen as contributing a kind of fixed spatial grid. Although height had been lost, depth displaced height and there still persisted fixed natures, especially human nature. In postmodernity however, neither height nor depth remains, but only a shifting surface flux, because immanence is now conceived in terms of the primacy of time, not space. Possibility, productivity, and change have been set free, both for nature and culture, which, as a result, are increasingly indistinguishable. It follows, of course, that both modernity and postmodernity are relentlessly secular — meaning by that (1) that they explain and evaluate without reference to transcendence, (2) that they see finite reality as self-explanatory and self-governing, and (3) that they see this finite reality which is the *saeculum* — the time before the eschaton for Christian theology — as being all that there is.

In these senses, postmodernity is not more open to religion than is modernity — indeed, as more emphatically immanentist, it is really less so. Nevertheless, just as there were strange modern modes of religiosity, so there are strange postmodern modes of religiosity. Two of these are worth mentioning. First of all, academic exponents of relatively Marxist versions of postmodernism are fond of giving a Spinozistic twist to their atheism. The plane of immanence is seen as the sphere of active, productive forces, which manifest themselves in human terms as desire and love: the still beckoning communist future is seen as an apocalyptic refusal of negative, resentful, tragic, and death-obsessed emotion as being unnecessary, and as hitherto imposed upon us by alien oppressors. Something of Spinoza's "intellectual love" or his *Deus Sive Natura* persists in all this — there is to be a joyful reception and active contemplation of the immanent totality. For indeed, once oppression is surpassed, liberated nature-going-beyond-nature fully appears.

MODERN   POST-MODERN

LIFE SUCKS   LIFE SUCKS

The second example is at a far more popular and widely dispersed level, and at first sight it seems quite different and perhaps not postmodern at all. This is the phenomenon of "new age religions." These religions all stress that salvation is to be located in a higher self, above the social, temporal, remembered self. This self can put one in harmony with everything, with the whole cosmos. This seems unpostmodern, to the extent that it takes modern individualism to an extreme and seems to advocate retreat within an absolutely private, interior space. But this position shares with the Spinozistic one an assumption of immanence — of a self-regulating cosmos. Moreover, its higher-self-merging-with-the-cosmos is really rather like the ironic remove of the Spinozistic subject from its own process in flux — it is akin also to the Wittgenstein of the *Tractatus,* able to speak of what belongs to the subject as somehow standing impossibly outside the "all" of things that can be spoken of. There are also parallels to Emmanuel Levinas and Jean-Luc Marion's tendency to demote the graspably visible world as the regime of totality, and to Michel Henry's proclamation of a world counter to this totality, which consists in the pure never visible interior of matter manifest as auto-affection.[2] Thus in postmodernity, alongside the stress of fluid and permeable boundaries, we have a new affirmation of the sanctity of an empty mystical self able to transcend, identity with, and promote or else refuse the totality of process in the name of a truer "life" which is invisible. It will be apparent that even organized religion gets infected today with this kind of "spirituality."

We need then to add the linked notions of immanence and self and life to the notions of nature merging with culture, of inside merging with outside, of information era and global regime, if we are to envisage the full dimensions of postmodernity.

Having sketched out the five dimensions, we now have to ask: How is the Church to manifest itself and articulate its position in these new circumstances? But clearly, there is a prior question: How is the Church to evaluate these circumstances? In answering both these questions, I want in general to suggest that we regard postmodernity, like modernity, as a kind of distorted outcome of energies first unleashed by the Church itself. If that is the case, then our attitude is

---

2. See John Milbank, "The Soul of Reciprocity: Parts One and Two," in *Modern Theology* (June and August, 2001).

bound to be a complex one. Not outright refusal, nor outright acceptance. More like an attempt at radical redirection of what we find. In recommending such a redirection, I suggest that neither a reiteration of Christian orthodoxy in identically repeated handed-down formulas nor a liberal adaptation to postmodern assumptions will serve as well. The latter response would clearly be a betrayal, but the former might well be betrayal of a more subtle kind — allowing us the illusion of a continuation of the faith in merely formal, empty terms that have discovered no real habitation for faith in our times, either with or against them. Instead, we must allow the very critical engagements with postmodernity to force us to re-express our faith in a radically strange way, which will carry with it a sense of real new discovery of the gospel and the legacy of Christian orthodoxy.

My assertion here is not intended as a general, methodological remark about Christianity in relation to culture, which might easily be taken as but another mode of liberalism. Instead, it is based upon the inevitable, if wary, affinity that must exist between Christianity and postmodernism. Postmodernism, I have said, is the obliteration of boundaries. And Christianity is the religion of the obliteration of boundaries. Secular commentators like Hardt and Negri assume, in all too modern and essential a fashion, that there is some sort of "natural" human desire that demands de-territorialization without end. I suggest, more cautiously, that Christianity itself invented a discourse and tradition of living beyond the law — and that the West is still thinking and living through this idea. For Christianity did, indeed, explode all limits: between nations, between races, between the sexes, between the household and the city, between ritual purity and impurity, between work and leisure, between days of the week, between sign and reality (in the sacraments), between the end of time and living in time, and even between culture and nature, since Jesus advised us to follow the mute example of the lilies of the field. Indeed the category "creature" enfolds and transcends both the natural and the cultural — culture for the Gospels is only a higher and more intense "life"; while, inversely, all of nature is the divine artifact. But above all, with the doctrine of the Incarnation, Christianity violates the boundary between created and creator, immanence and transcendence, humanity and God. In this way, the arch taboo grounding all the others is broken.

However, there is an apparent problem here. Judaism (and the religion of the Old Testament also) is *not* the religion of the obliteration of boundaries. Indeed it is perhaps the very opposite: the religion of the reassertion of boundaries. Primitive cultures are marked by a rigid marking out of limits, often described as "taboos."[3] Later, when the societies are captured by state formations, taboos are removed, or else subordinated to more abstract laws that are imposed from outside, not inscribed in ritual practice. Ancient Israel, however, appears to have reacted against state formations like Egypt and Babylon, by making a kind of half-return to the primitive, and inventing a new system of more universalized ritual boundaries. All the primitive tribal boundaries had to do with restricting complexity, confusion, and so conflict. But while they are thus comprehensible in functional terms, the actual instances of taboo can often seem utterly arbitrary. The provisions of the *Torah*, by contrast, although often strange-seeming, exhibit a more cosmic scope and a more unrestricted interest in limiting the shedding of blood, and the confusion of categories that could lead to instability and struggle. It is as if the Jewish people took up, in a more universal mode, the instinctive sense of all primitive peoples that barriers must be erected against future danger and the augmentation of human and natural power.

Are we to take it, then, that Christianity really reverses this mission of Israel to the world? But such an interpretation is forbidden to us by all Patristic teaching. To take this view would be at once to side wholeheartedly with postmodernity, and to refuse, as the work of a demiurge, the revelation of the old covenant. Postmodernity, not Christianity, is the final refusal of all taboo, and it is worth mentioning here the Jewish anthropologist Franz Steiner's suggestion that the Jews were destroyed by the Nazis not — as for Emmanuel Levinas — in the name of totality, but rather as the people of the limit, in the name of the transgression of every limit, by immanent crowned power.

So are we here presented with some sort of clue to the riddle of our times? Some thread through the postmodern labyrinth? Is postmodernity the misreading of the gospel's beyond the law? Does it overstress the passing beyond boundaries at the expense of the virtue

---

3. See Franz Baermann Steiner, *Selected Papers: Taboo* (New York: Berghahn, 1998) and *Selected Papers: Orientalism, Value and Civilization* (New York: Berghahn, 1998). I am indebted greatly to conversations on these matters with Michael Mack.

of boundaries? And does the cure for our postmodern condition lie in a healing of the rift between the seemingly opposed Christian and Jewish principles? Or rather does it lie in rediscovering that the Christian going beyond-the-law nonetheless preserves and elevates the law? This would mean nothing less than discovering a hidden mean between process and limit, between movement and stasis — in theological terms, the co-belonging of grace with law, and not a dialectical duality of law and gospel.

It is this clue which I now want to follow up in terms of the church's response to the five aspects of postmodernity. First of all, the question of the merging of nature and culture.

Religious people tend, instinctively, to feel uneasy in the face of a general collapse of all that was once regarded as natural. They are tempted to fall back on an insistence that God has made the human species and all others to be as they should be, and that either nature, or God's positive law, has given clear and firm guidance for the conduct of human sexual relations and reproduction. The trouble with this approach, though, is that an open-ended transformation of the natural world has always been regarded by Christian theology as proper to our *humanum,* and even as intrinsic to the redemption of humanity and the cosmos, looking towards the *eschaton.* Already, throughout history, we have drastically altered both nature and our bodies, and questions of right and wrong here have never been decidable *merely* in terms of what has been pre-given by divine design. Certainly, that must be ceaselessly attended to, but questions of right and wrong in those instances more ultimately require a discernment of teleology, and a ceaseless discrimination of what is good in itself.

Here it needs to be said that the Renaissance unleashing of a sense of human creativity along with one of the undeveloped potentials of natural forces did not automatically go along with a loss of a sense of teleology and of participation in God. The new sense of creativity and power was not at all simply the counterpart, as Gilles Deleuze and Antonio Negri tend to claim, of Scotist univocity, which encouraged thinkers to speak, for the first time, of finite being *qua* being without reference to God. Instead, one can see that alternative interpretations were offered of human creativity, in terms *either* of univocity *or* analogy. In terms of univocity, human creativity is taken to mean that, in a certain domain — for example, politics or mathematics or even physics (as with Galileo) — human beings have, univocally, the same kind and extension of power as God has. It is *this* interpretation that engenders what Hans von Balthasar called "Titanism." In terms of analogy, however, as especially worked out by Nicholas of Cusa, who thought still within a Dionysian perspective, human creative power and natural power are never equal to God, and yet in their very creative exercise participate in the divine *Logos* or *Ars,* and register "conjecturally" a sense of how things should develop towards their proper goals. Even in its originating, creativity remains discerning.

When it comes to contemporary practical examples, we need to continue to exercise this power of discernment. For example, surrogate father- or motherhood is not wrong because it violates the pregiven process of reproduction. Rather, we have to ask very complex questions about what such procedures will do to human identity — and whether the different identities that may thereby emerge are richer or weaker identities, more viable or else more unstable and threatened. Ultimately, we have to ask whether the co-belonging of sex and procreation alone sustains human beings as more than commodities, because they are thereby the outcome of personal encounters at once both accidental and yet chosen, in a fashion that is irreplaceable, and essential to an ontological grammar that we should continue to elect. (I believe the answer is yes.) But such reflections involve not a refusal of choice, nor a mere postmodern resignation to choice, but a kind of higher-level "choice about choice." At present, of course, we woefully lack cultural practices that might mediate our intersubjective metachoices.

At present, the postmodern fusion of nature with culture is more like the collapse of nature into culture. The Christian question here might be as to whether this emphasis should be reversed. That is to suggest that while we accept and embrace the revisability of the given world, this dynamism needs and should not refuse notions of nature and essence, not as what is exhaustively given but as what may eventually be disclosed with and through time, rather than despite it. Certain transformations and graftings may develop and unfold more of a partially pre-given and desirable identity; certain others, the reverse. Certain hybrids should find their place; certain others not. Certain interventions within the rhythms of nature still permit and uphold them; certain others run a clear if incalculable risk of upsetting them. It is all a matter of discernment, according to no prewritten rules, pre-

cisely because we have faith that we do live in a creation where discernment is possible. In this sense, the transgression of boundaries is not antinomic, because it is rather the ceaseless extension of the book of the law in real positive enactments.

The contesting of the postmodern lies precisely in this trust in discernment and the discrimination amongst resting places. Postmodernity inscribes, tyrannically, only one law: produce, alter, or make different, such that yesterday's transgressive innovation is today's crime of stasis. In this sense its antinomianism enacts a new law and is not, like the gospel, really beyond the law at all. For if there is truly no essence or nature, no "proper way" for anything to be, then nothing should be attended to, nothing should be regarded in its hidden possibilities for its *own* development; rather, every possibility must imply that its realization requires an act of arbitrary (and not at all creative) destruction. Certain Spinozistically inclined postmodernists are fond of speaking of the extension of bonds of love and solidarity on the basis of compatible emotions and understandings.[4] But this is to invoke the primacy of *affinity*, and there can be affinity only between things that can be in some fashion *characterized*, even if such characterization is provisional. Otherwise there are only affinities of accident, whose instances convey no freight of enacted truth, and which instantiate no proleptic hope of a final chain of affinities with no exterior of exclusion. (Indeed, given the Spinozistic rooting of passive resentment in the limited perspectives of the finite modes, there must always be exclusion, save for the privileged attainment of the active perspective of the absolute by a fated few.) Furthermore, without the *convenientia* of analogy, the binding of differences under affinity can be no more than a merging and coalescence into a single superdifference.

The gospel concerns, above all for us today, this issue of affinity. For Christians, God became man and denied the division between creator and creation. However, in doing so, he also preserved it. God, in becoming man, in no way changed in himself, in no way entered within time — to claim that he did so would be, as it were, theologically anti-Semitic and antinomian. Nor was anything that Christ did in any way "mixed" with his divinity — except at one point — namely

---

4. See, for example, Michael Hardt, *Gilles Deleuze* (Minneapolis: Minnesota University Press, 1997).

that of personality, or of character. Jesus was God because his *affinity* with God was so extreme as to constitute identity — although an identity not of substantial nature, but of character, *hypostasis, persona*. And Jesus communicated to his disciples not simply teaching, but precisely this *character*, which they were to repeat differently, so constituting a community of affinity with Jesus. Not a community of nature — not a family — nor a coerced association — a *polis* — nor yet a postmodern market proliferation of differences. Rather a community of differences in identity — but an identity diffused through the non-identical repetition of character, or of affinity. Affinity is the absolutely non-theorizable; it is the ineffable. Affinity is the sacred. And it is the beyond-the-ethical that alone gives us the ethical, for without affinity, love can only be the merely ethical and immanent command to put the other first — a self-abasement before the rival egotism of the other — which she would in turn have to renounce. Instead of modern selfishness, one would then have a kind of postmodern endless postponement of egotism (Levinas and Derrida). By contrast, there can only be more than egotism, there can only be *love* — if there is ecstatic reciprocity and interplay of characters who naturally "belong together." In this way, the network of affinity, beyond nature, discovers a higher nature (the supernatural, the gift of grace). It is for this reason that loving God, in the Bible, involves not just our being well disposed towards God, but being "like" God, akin to God, made in his image. This image does not fundamentally consist in any single human property — our reason alone, for example, abstracted from all other aspects — but rather in the whole person (even if this be specifically a whole rational person). Thus we cannot say *in what respect* we are like God — the image simply is an ineffable likeness: an affinity.

I think that lack of trust in affinity, lack of the mediation of affinity through the Church might, to a degree, explain the *sexual* crises and confusions of our time. However, Christians can say this only with fear and trembling, because throughout much of their history and yet much more especially in the period since the Reformation, they have failed to realize that affinity puts the erotic at the heart of *agapē*, which cannot be merely the empty and nihilistic gaze of well-wishing. Because affinity, having a liking for someone, falling in love, etc. seems uncontrollable — as indeed they are — we have tended to think they are non-moral or unmoralizable spheres — whereas to the contrary, these phenomena are the very preconditions for morality. Without ontological kinship — a kind of aesthetic co-belonging of some with some, and so ultimately of all with all, not formally and indifferently (as if every person were equally near every other, as on the Internet, which not accidentally is awash with prostitution in multiple guises) but via the mediation of degrees of preference — there can be no possibility of real peace and reconciliation, only a kind of suspension of hostilities.

For these sorts of reasons, I think we are totally wrong to approach contemporary sexual issues as primarily a moral matter, or of what should and should not be done. On the whole, disagreements about sexual morality are a farcical unreality, masking grotesque depths of hypocrisy. "Liberals" always seek more fidelity and security than they own up to; "conservatives," in practice, will usually put life before principle. In this realm, the sham of argument is forever overshadowed and defeated by anxiety. So the Church should forthwith cease its participation in these unedifying disputes. Marriage is not a matter of morality, but of the basis of morality in occurrence. It is either there or not there — entirely willed by the partners and by them alone, only because God himself has joined them together. This is Christ's teaching, and like him we should keep ironic and blushing silence about everything else, and leave it to the discernment of individuals and pastoral guidance. Equally horrendous are the conservative attack on "sex outside marriage" (with no real warrant in Christian tradition — especially lay tradition) and the "liberal" slandering of fidelity, which is a slandering of sexuality itself and its deeply ethical jealousies. This same slandering fails to observe the increasing displacement of erotic affinity by a general system of market competition for sexual conquest that is entirely complicit with the pursuit of economic power and advantage (as the French novelist Alain Houillebecq has demonstrated). Both liberals and conservatives also tend to perpetuate the ludicrous untruth that erotic excitement and fulfillment increase with the new and the altogether strange, and lapse with time and familiarity. Yet to the contrary, common experience proves that sex is impossible save in the relaxed presence of the ever-different-familiar, even if familiarity can descend from the outset, like a miracle. Freedom, innovation, and passion grow here most surely with custom alone, as much as in the exchange of words, musical notes, or witticisms. It is not that sex outside marriage is wrong; simply that it is impossible, and never what anyone wants in the slightest.

It should in addition be said here that modernity, specifically (ever since the Renaissance), has always oscillated in sexual matters, between a disciplinary puritanism unknown to the Middle Ages, on the one hand, and a promotion of a dark, death-obsessed, and narcissistic eroticism, on the other. Often postmodernity accentuates the latter path, but here once again, it privileges entirely the flow of difference over the fertile pools of relatively constant essence. In particular, it tends to despise the mystery of the general difference of masculine and feminine, in favor of a supposedly more exciting dispersed and unpolar differentiation. Yet this ungeneric, ungendered, and so of course unsexual differentiation, cannot then truly allow any arrival of the event of affinity in its most intense sexual mode, since it thereby lacks any vehicle of mediation. Male/female sexual difference, while it is indeed mysterious and sublimely ineffable, nevertheless does not entirely escape articulation — else it would be a vacuous difference that made no difference. In general, the clichés truly do hold, although they must be further nuanced forever: men are more nomadic, direct, and abstractive; women are more settled, subtle, and particularizing — though they are both equally innovative, legislative, and conservative within these different modes. A preponderance of counter-instances could of course be held to disprove this assertion, yet equally they could be held to witness to the abolition of gender by a ruthless postmodern capitalism that wishes to engender only "individuals" turned narcissistically to themselves and to the abstract center, never to the embodied other who displays a radical generic otherness that truly unsettles our egoity. The same abolition requires the ideal synthesis of "masculine" autonomy and self-control, with "feminine" compliance and sociability (these traditional qualities being somewhat more culturally induced, one might argue). It desires neither men nor women. None of this can be "proved," but it is often important to state boldly what one sees and cannot in the nature of the case demonstrate: this is the real crux of responsibility. And the issue in the end concerns not bald fact, but rather the question of what is really desirable — an equality of the sexes without sexual difference (and an *entirely* inexpressible difference is no difference, even if one must struggle forever to articulate it), or a new equality of the sexes that seeks to enhance a sexual difference that it also affirms — teleologically and eschatologically.

Equality of difference: without the settled, abstraction is not an abstraction but only another arbitrary, settled view. While inversely, without abstraction the settled is not settled, but another abstraction in its very fixity — immune to the specific shifts of life and time. (Here also Christian abstraction is necessarily betrothed to Jewish specificity.) Instead, without this marriage, we are speaking of multiple narcissisms and purely active and so self-expressive desires without need and lack (for lack can persist non-negatively within fulfillment). This kind of sexuality is "transcendentally homosexual," and this must be the outcome, where male-female relations are not seen as paradigmatic of the sexual as such. There need be no problem whatsoever with the idea that homosexual practice is part of the richness of God's creation or that its non-heterosexual logic (with which two enamored partners may share a desire for a third)[5] can hint towards the life of angels, but where homosexuality is seen as equal in human (rather than cosmic) sacramental significance to the unity in difference of man and woman (where it is supposed that people of the same sex can "marry" — although we need other rites for same-sex unions) then as a matter of logic, one has chosen the superiority of homosexuality over heterosexuality, and denied the place of the non-angelic within the cosmic and erotic order. If both are "the same," then, indeed, "the same" triumphs: transcendentally speaking, there are simply many "persons," all in theory potential sexual partners. It seems that there can be no "neutral" characterization of sexuality as such: one has to choose — even if what seems subordinate *qua* human gestures more specifically toward the higher angelic order.

In fact it is heterosexuality and sexual difference that the Church finds *really* difficult to accept — though it lies at the very heart of its mystery. Thus it was persecuted by the old Puritanism and is now denied by the new pious indifference towards gender, for which all that matters is "friendship." Far too easily, and with a sham radicalism, the churches and especially the clergy tend to degenerate into secret gay cults: the gnosis of campdom. After all, the homoerotic has dominated them for centuries: what is new, exciting, or radical about any of this? Today, past patriarchy and misogyny are on occasion writ larger and more explicitly within circles of male gay hegemony. In addition, the production of a normative "homosexual" subjectivity serves, as Theodor Adorno rightly foresaw, the deepest purposes of capitalism:

5. Howls of protest here are futile: these things are again and again observable.

thereby the production of children can be increasingly commodified and handed over to state and market regulation, so that human beings may be the better subordinated to the increase of profit and the stock-piling of abstract power. No, the test of its real embracing of incarnate mystery will come when the Church is able to accept and no longer to trivialize human sexuality in its most shocking, vivid, and defining (heterosexual) guise.

In the face of the fusing of nature and culture, therefore, the church should proclaim the "gospel of affinity." It is the Church of all the marriages and quasi-marriages, the church of all natural and spiritual offspring. Appropriate responses to other aspects of post-modernity then follow from this central insight. In the face of the blending of private and public, the church needs to accentuate the private pole as the underplayed one, as earlier it identified that of nature. Since the church fuses *oikos* and *polis,* values of nurture and reconciliation need to constitute our interweavings, not locked doors, barren highways, and dangerous animals. We must learn to take literally the idea that we are "grafted" into Israel, that we now belong with Israel in one spiritual blood group, and we must think of all our human relations in terms of extended family. The computer screen makes us equally near the whole world — but we need to resist the illusion that this is possible. We are finite and we cannot love all equally, except in loving God and trusting that those other people are also loved. We need rather to love properly those that we are destined to love. And such extensions of family must invade also the entire realm of law and punishment. The church should promote the sense that such processes must be processes of penance and reconciliation as well as of justice. It must have done forever with Luther's two kingdoms, and the notion that a state that does not implicitly concern itself with the soul's salvation can be in any way legitimate.

Therefore reconciliation needs to be added to affinity. In the face of the information age, the church needs — thirdly — to be wary of the secular tendency to promote the abstract, and should come to realize that only Christianity fully celebrates the concrete and bodily. For if the immanent world is all there is, then it tends to reduce to our abstract grasp of it, and we come to believe that it consists in these rearrangeable abstractions. For this outlook, there is neither being, nor knowledge, nor the affinity between them, but rather a shifting flux of the semi-concrete and the semi-abstract (the realm first located by Duns Scotus in terms of the formal distinction).[6] By contrast, we are able to acknowledge a depth in things only when we see them as surpassing our finite grasp, and as grounded in God the Creator. In this way only a recognition of participation in God gives bodies their solidity, because to grant them this we need to see how in God bodies persist as eternal. Likewise, we have true knowledge of them only when we share something of God's insight into how he wished them to be. So if an overabstracting secular world has lost bodies and truth in favor of information, we need to reclaim both those realities. With Spinoza this time, we need to develop a less ascetic spirituality and insist that to participate more in God, we need always to enter further into true, temperate, corporeal pleasures. The insinuation of both puritans and atheists that one must choose either sensual pleasure *or* God, always sacrificing either one or the other, must be exposed as a reduction of God to the ontic: considering him as if he were a finite recompense for the loss of something finite.

So we now have affinity, reconciliation, and embodiment. In the face of globalization and the new American empire, we need to counterpose Augustine's counter-empire, the city of God. We may do this alongside many secular brethren: socialists, communists, and anarchists. We should not refuse their cooperation, but yet we should insist that they have little real grasp of the counter-empire, since for them it is still a matter of simply unleashing more undifferentiated liberty, going yet further beyond the law. For us, rather, it should seem that the impossibility of pure flux and unmediated difference will inevitably bring with it only an arbitrary and oppressive de-territorialization. The only way, by contrast, to escape restricting terrain is to refuse even the opposition of territory and escape. If there *is* any human nature, perhaps it resides in the desire to be at once at home and abroad. But this is possible only where one admits the lure of transcendence. For then both immanent dynamism and immanent stasis are both outplayed; then the flux is not itself an immanent God — the pure space of pure movement — but consists only in the relay stations, the open but identifiable essences along its course. Then we are not postmodern nomads, but ecclesial pilgrims.

So to affinity, reconciliation, and embodiment we can now add not only the city of God but also transcendence. Immanence appears to be

---

6. See Catherine Pickstock, *After Writing* (Oxford: Blackwell, 1998), pp. 121-67.

democratic and mobile, but it always re-erects a hierarchy of self-government that sunders the totality between the static and the mobile, or else the other way around. If the mobile is on top, as in postmodernity, then, of course, its truth can never arrive in the world, and the postmodern or new-age self perceiving this truth is ironically removed from the world and its real selfhood of memory and hope. We can then never be liberated, nor redeemed. No gift will ever be given. Instead, since pure flux, pure de-territorialization, will never be manifest, the urge towards this illusion will always engender the surrogate of formal, arbitrary, and oppressive control of the flux by a sovereign empire. By contrast, transcendence appears hierarchic and fixed, but its ontological height is beyond all immanent heights, and therefore is as close to ontic depths as to ontic elevations. For this reason, its truth *can* be mediated to us and we *can*, one day, be liberated. For this reason, transcendence offers us its gift of affinity through reconciliation, in our bodies on pilgrimage within the city of God below.

What Is a Post-Christian?

ROBERT W. JENSON

Obviously, my use of the prefix "post" follows a vogue. I use the prefix in one of its somewhat more recent senses, as follows. First, to be "post"-something is to be that something no longer, but not yet to be anything else either, and so to be determined precisely by what one is no longer. Second, the something one is no longer is a communal something and only so an individual something. Thus to be post-Christian is to belong to a community — a polity or civil society — which used to be Christian and whose habits of thought and policies of action are determined by that very fact. One can therefore be a post-Christian without knowing anything about Christianity — and many in the West's great cities are now in just that condition.

I will begin by relying on the greatest single authority in the matter: the Rev. Father Brown, the detective priest of G. K. Chesterton's mystery stories. According to Father Brown, a society that runs modernity out to its end condemns itself above all to proliferating superstition. I cite a rebuke to a young secularist friend, from the collection *The Incredulity of Father Brown:* "It's drowning all your . . . rationalism and skepticism, it's coming in like a sea; and the name of it is superstition. . . . It's the first effect of not believing in God that you lose your common sense and can't see things as they are. Anything that anybody talks about, and says there's a good deal in it, extends itself indefinitely like a vista in a nightmare. And a dog is an omen, and a cat is a mystery. . . . All the menagerie of polytheism [returns]: dog Anubis and great green-eyed Pasht and all the holy howling bulls of

Bashan, reeling back to the bestial gods of the beginning . . . , and all because you are frightened of four words, 'He was made man'."

Religiously, a post-Christian culture will be, according to Father Brown, above all a credulous culture, a culture that in moral and religious matters lacks a compass. And a post-Christian individual will be someone deprived, perhaps through no fault of his or her own, of that vital device.

It is important to note that it is recoil from the specifically *Christian,* triune God that has this effect. It is refusal to say "He was made man" on cultural turf once shaped by its saying, that delivers us to repristinated superstition. It is not possible to disbelieve generically, since it is not possible to believe generically. As Schleiermacher surely showed once and for all, there is no such thing as generic religion, only a generic propensity to be religious, in one or another specific way. Thus, as it is only possible to believe some particular religion, so it is only possible to reject or abandon some particular religion. Becoming post-Buddhist or post-animist would doubtless have its specific effects also, but what these may be is not our concern here. On the authority of Father Brown, it is recoil from the God who was made man, the triune God, that opens the sea of superstition.

I do have to modify Father Brown's position at two points. First, we should perhaps note explicitly what he does not: that in our civilization the affiliation of secularized reason and superstition goes back to the very beginning of secularized reason. The great century of so-called Enlightenment, the eighteenth, was also a great century of practiced witchcraft and of general belief in its efficacy, of preposterous but unquestioned medical quackery, and of charlatanisms in every field, of religions invented on the spur of enthusiasm, of "magnetisms" and spiritualisms and materialisms in endless variety.

The Enlightenment trusted in the new science and its supposed empiricism to distinguish truth from error. But while science within itself is indeed steered by more or less stringent controls, among which are occasional checks by observation, these controls are hardly adapted to distinguish faith from superstition, aesthetic insight from foppery, or morality from prejudice; and relying on them to do so only opens a boundless field of arbitrary preference. Histories of revolutionary Paris, the great laboratory of the Enlightenment, if they tell of more than official political history, reveal a period in which the stuff of public discourse was utterly implausible ideological assertion, quite immune to even the most blatant empirical or rational disconfirmation. It is no original observation of mine: whatever moral or aesthetic or religious compass modernity has had was always provided by the cultural residue of Christianity, and it is modernity's progressive elimination of even the residue that now delivers us wholly to superstition.

Second, and more important to my argument, Father Brown seems to think that the old gods can and will come back in their original character, that we will actually revert to the gods of "the beginning." Here, surely, he is wrong, perhaps misled by too dismissive an understanding of the old gods. The Goddess promoted in decadent modernity is not the primeval deity; she is all too plainly but a pitiable bowdlerization of that great appearance: she is precisely an artifact of superstition. The grim old Goddess herself could certainly not have been recruited to the cause of women's rights or even of women's humanity, she being dead set against them; it was her very deity to open to any male who would have her — or to slay him — or both. The philosophically unreflected cult of Vishnu at an Indian temple, carried by people immemorially born to that temple, is one thing — and a noble thing, with whose authenticity Christian theology must somehow reckon; the cult of Vishnu carried by dropouts and Hollywood gentry is something else.

For the great effect that Christianity leaves behind it, where it has come and has departed, is a vacuum where an antecedent mythology had been. This was much discussed in my theological youth, under the label of "secularization theology," most profoundly by Friedrich Gogarten in his great book *Der Mensch zwischen Gott und Welt*. It was the insight of this movement that the gospel, and indeed the general impact of Scripture, stripped the world of its divine aura and restored it to its true reality as wonderful creature, rather than ambivalently fructifying and menacing divinity. Consider only the opening verses of Genesis. With the Earth-Goddess, the "host of heaven" was the other primary object of ancient religion; Genesis reduces that host to lamps and clocks the Lord made and hung up there for the general convenience.

I was convinced of the truth of this secularization-thesis then and remain convinced now. And from the beginning of my work I have worried about what would happen to a culture once deprived by Scripture of its mythology, when, as plainly seemed to be happening, it thereupon abandoned the Scriptures also.

Thus it is possible to regard Scripture's demythologizing of the world as a good thing or as a bad thing. Philosophers of science tend to regard it as a good, or indeed indispensable thing. The recent "deep ecology" movement and various Christian dissenters of course have regarded it as a bad thing. Those who are unwilling to say "And was made man," and are willing to take the gods of the beginning as better than nothing, try vainly to reverse secularization. All I can say here is that if we think Scripture's demythologizing of the creation a bad thing, then we think Judaism and Christianity bad and should put our affiliations where our opinions are.

Note that I do not say that where the gospel goes it undoes antecedent "myths" but that it undoes antecedent "mythology." A mythology is not a grab-bag of numina and stories about them; it is precisely a *logos* of images and stories: it is a coherent account of reality and of the life appropriate thereto. It is the myths' *logos* that the gospel undoes, by attacking every mythology's primary grammatical presupposition, that "in my end is my beginning," that the story of reality is a story of how it was in the beginning and therefore always is and therefore blessedly always will be.

For in the Scriptures, things are *not* now as they were in the beginning. And the kingdom to which the Scriptures point will be neither how it was in the beginning nor how it now is.

How things now are, is fallen from their beginning. It has been argued that the doctrine of the fall has slender biblical basis, in that the Old Testament, where we should expect to find it, has no doctrine of a fall. But that is only because critical scholars have until recently looked for it in the wrong place. The story of actual Israel, as against the story of pre-Israel told in Genesis, begins with the Exodus, and here we find that no sooner is the covenant established than it is broken, and that this brokenness determines the whole subsequent history of Israel. It is always in the light of Exodus that we should read the stories of its antecedents, including the first chapters of Genesis; and when we do this we will find Paul's interpretation of Genesis 3, which became the church's traditional interpretation, not far off the mark.

Moreover, the biblical story of the beginning itself points to a fulfillment beyond itself, with or without a fall. In one way, the creation is there in the work of the six days; but in another way it is not, for there is a seventh day for God to "rest," and for the creatures in his image to sanctify in their own way. The flow of the text is clear: this seventh day beyond creation determines creation. On each of the six days it is said that the creatures of that day are "good." We are intended to ask "Good for what?" At least part of the answer is provided: good for the seventh day's holiness beyond making, even by God.

Thus the faith of Israel, and so of the church, is eschatological, independently of particular passages of her Scripture or particular developments in her religious history. Scripture does not find the truth of things in what they have been and therefore are, but in what they will be beyond themselves, that is, in what they will be in God, for God is all there is beyond creatures.

So when we westerners now summon back Father Brown's "gods of the beginning," their proper *logos* is no longer there to accommodate them, for the gospel has debunked it. But these numina have reality only within some general *logos*, some grammar assumed fitted to reality. The gospel not being hospitable to them, and their original *logos* now having been discredited, two *logoi* offer themselves.

Nihilism offers itself. If, as Christianity has made us see, the world is not holy, perhaps nothing is — the amphiboly is intended. Nihilism, if it were actually achieved, would be the apprehension of sheer emptiness — in religious terms, sheer secularity — as what encompasses and enables and terminates all things. Its doctrine is that the being of beings is their non-being, the purpose of life death. From Jean-Paul's *"Reden des toten Christus vom Weltall herab,"* through Nietzsche, through Heidegger in some moods, through Nietzsche's and Heidegger's sad French and American epigones, modernity has been replete with nihilism's prophets. With glee or horror or with both at once, they have announced the advent of a time when it would not be possible to believe in anything, or what despite the formal fallacy is the same thing, it would be possible and necessary to believe in nothingness.

Now it may well be doubted that it is possible to be an actual nihilist, since as Camus observed, even suicide itself is an intentional act, and is thus self-contradictory. But it is evidently possible to live by the expectation of nihilism, since many have in fact done and do so, most spectacularly of course such as the German National Socialists, or the Stalinist and post-Stalinist *nomenklatura* or, say, the planned parenthood movement or the Hemlock Society.

And in such, perhaps subliminal, anticipation, multitudes live *as if* they were nihilists, often, in keeping with my earlier observation about the communal nature of the phenomenon, through little fault of their own. One will of course mention the *Lumpenproletariat* of the reservations, rural or urban, but can just as well instance the endlessly generated new multi-millionaires of the finance-casino, who find nothing to do with their lives but spend eighteen hours a working day making money and weekends trying desperately to get rid of it.

Now — the Father Brownian point to be made is that almost-nihilists are bound to be religious, in a certain way. It is the "almost" in "almost-nihilism" that will be filled up with religion.

The mark of almost-nihilism's religiosity is that it is made up, and known by its devotees to be made up. It is nihilistic religiosity in that its objects are known to be — nothing. To observe such arbitrary religious invention happening, you need only attend that remarkable caricature of the American religious scene, the annual national convention of the American Academy of Religion, most sessions of which will be devoted to considering what parts of what "traditions" can be crafted together to make a religion satisfactory to some group and/or set of interests. All the "bestial gods of the beginning" are indeed inspected for what use we might make of them, i.e., what role they might play in our superstition, while the more conservative handle Christian "symbols" and "metaphors" and "concerns" in just the same way. It is important to realize that these self-appointed religious founders-out-of-nothing are quite aware and deliberate about what they are doing. Or merely consider how the teachings and rites of our churches are often treated by their supposed members, as a smorgasbord from which to assemble each their religion to taste, often enough again making it quite explicit that this is what they are doing.

Do the members of even such invented religions as demand commitment leading to suicide or dementia think that their doctrines are actually *about* anything? It seems all too apparent that they do not. Or how are we to construe the spiritual life of members of mainline Christian denominations, who happily recite the Nicene Creed, yet queried in other contexts respond that of course no one anymore thinks the Resurrection, for example, really happened? If nothing is true, anything is true and I say what I please when I say it. "Do I contradict myself? Very well, I contradict myself." Do I believe simultaneously that abortion is the taking of a human life and that this should be done by individual "choice"? Very well, I believe these simultaneously.

The other *logos* available to provide grammar for the returning "bestial" gods is what we may call abstracted Christianity, Christianity bereft of the particularity of Christ and so turned into ideology. Most "progressive" Christianity is of this sort.

Here we may think, for instance, of a doctrine powerful in our culture, that all religions lead to the same place. This is by no means newly imported by such explicitly superstitious types as John Hick, but has been among us at least since Emerson and is now a nearly unquestioned orthodoxy. What one must see is that the doctrine as practiced assumes that the "place" to which all religions lead is the one *Christianity* taught us to look forward to. What is done is to take a folk-piety version of Christ's kingdom, abstract Christ from it, and label the result with that dismal abstraction, "salvation." Then one can plug in as savior the Invisible Hand or Brahman or the Goddess or a cute tribal fetish or the channeled voice of your own dead grandmother, or whatever. Or we may think of the remarkably implausible but widespread supposition that there is such a thing as "theism," of which Christianity is a variety but of which there are other varieties as well, necessarily with at least partly interchangeable parts.

It would be possible to argue that abstracted Christianity was the whole project of modernity. Christianity claimed to tell a universally encompassing story, a "metanarrative" if you will, and posited as a correlated notion the universal possibility of finding one's place in the narrative. Modernity appropriated the claim and the posit, hoping to maintain the form of the Christian story without telling it about Christ. The universal possibility of finding one's place in the truth was abstracted to become the posit of a formal rationality universally possessed, which was then to discover and construe the universal story.

To hindsight, the project appears rather obviously doomed. It was the attempt to have a universal story without the universal storyteller, an attempt that had either immediately to face its own absurdity or openly or covertly cast *us* in the role of universal storytellers. One has to say that we tried hard to fill the role, but finally were not up to it. The project crashed at the turn of the last century with what in the visual arts and music was called "modernism" and elsewhere has come to be called "*post*modernism."

Yet though modernity's project may have crashed, those among the ex-Christians who are not quite ready merely to await nihilism have found nothing to replace it. For the most part, we moderns who also want to be somehow religious soldier on with abstracted Christianity. Thereby we but maintain a welcoming *logos* for Father Brown's returning gods.

That "we" is to be noted in this connection. To the precise extent that American denominational Christianity missed out on the theological revolutions of the 1920s, and so carries on with modernity's project in the midst of modernity's demise, much of American Christianity has itself become post-Christian. Who is a post-Christian? Well — there are whole immense congregations, of all denominations or none, that are post-Christian at least in their public self-presentation. Their theology is a collection of clichéd abstractions — "love" and "acceptance" and "empowerment" and "peace-and-justice" (one word), and so on — and they could easily make any hero or mythic figure at all be the loving or accepting or empowering one, or the guru of peace-and-justice, instead of Jesus, and sometimes do.

It will have become evident that so far as daily behavior is concerned, the nihilistic and abstract-Christian versions of superstition are likely to work out to much the same thing: isolated individual or collective subjects, adrift in moral space, grab bits and pieces from a religious smorgasbord, to make each his, her, or its religion. Under various terms of analysis, the phenomenon itself has been often observed: as "consumer religion" or "lay liberalism" or "demotic gnosticism." Father Brown had the best label: "superstition."

Driving through a territory seemingly without FM stations the other day, Blanche and I switched to AM and encountered Dr. Laura, whom we had never heard before. We could not tear our ears from the aimless religiosity and utter moral confusion so cheerily displayed — "Hi, Dr. Laura." "Hi, Jennifer." Here was the woman with one child by her boyfriend before they were married and now another after they have married, whose "very traditional" father- and mother-in-law persist in disapproving of her, a situation described in the purest babble of "abuse" and "challenge" and "acceptance." She and her husband, she says, are "very spiritual," not that they practice any religion but that they like to read about various religious things and experiment with some of them, and she thinks that may be part of "the challenge" she presents to her father-in-law. And here was Dr. Laura, dispensing the most disastrous moral and religious advice right off the top of her head.

Or consider a couple of things in the *Times* recently. There was the picture of the outside advert board of a Methodist congregation in the Carolinas, offering drop-by communion for commuters, between 6 and 8. And there was a wedding announcement according to which Presbyterian minister so-and-so would perform the "non-denominational" service.

So what are the churches to do? How are we to evangelize post-Christians? According to its title, my essay should be purely descriptive and diagnostic, but I am really not up to such asceticism.

First, we must purge our churches themselves of almost-nihilism and abstracted Christianity. Or rather, we must pray God to purge us of them, for we plainly are not going to do it voluntarily.

If God is thus merciful, our churches will of course get much smaller than they are. It is all very well to denounce such theologians as Stanley Hauerwas for "sectarianism," but they have much the right of it against their critics, though my own diagnosis is perhaps somewhat more relativist than theirs. Whether the church is to be a massive and accepted presence in the world, and necessarily then in some measure continuous with the world, or is to be a small and clearly delineated polity and civil society of its own, depends in my view on its calling in a time and place. When Constantine, speaking for a dying antiquity, called the church to be the moral and intellectual restorer of late Mediterranean civilization, I do not see how the church could have refused this service of love. But equally, as the West now defines itself against the faith, the church only perverts herself when she tries to hang on to her Constantinian position, by bowing and scraping to the culture. And in this connection, by the way, we must pray to be spared the European outcome, where the churches have become smaller indeed, but only cling the more desperately to their illusions.

We also need to face another fact often spoken of but rarely acted upon: that the West is now a mission field. We can no longer count on the culture doing half our work for us. On a mission field, the church has to do its own work, and that means first of all that it has to know precisely what is *not* there in the culture, that it hopes to bring to it. Which is to say: it must know and cultivate its difference from that culture. All that talk a few years ago about the world setting the agenda, about seeing where God was at work in the world and jumping in to help, etc., was just a last gasp of the church's establishment in the West, of its erstwhile ability to suppose that what the culture nurtured as good had to be congruent with the good the church had to bring.

But these are generalities that apply to any missionary situation. What is specific to the church's situation in a post-Christian mission field?

We may take one step without distinguishing almost-nihilism and abstracted Christianity. Evangelism in the late-modern or postmodern West means rescuing our fellows from superstition, to worship the true God. At some times and places in the history of the church's mission, the religion and theology she finds antecedently in place are worthy of great respect, and the proper maxim may indeed be that here the gospel does not abolish what it finds but perfects it. Superstition, however, is simply an evil and must be dealt with as such. As we would hope to rescue someone from prostitution or drug addiction or marital abuse, so we must regard our mission to the devotees of "spirituality," the believers in all religions at once, the practitioners of magic, the amiable would-be skeptics in our residual congregations. Their errors are not foibles, or points of attachment for better religion, they are bondages to powers and principalities. They are to be argued against; their destructive power is to be pointed out to their victims in their own lives; the scare-instances of Moloch and Astarte and the Dialectic of History are to be limned.

As Father Brown knew, in a culture once Christian, the only alternative to superstition is "He became man." There is in the world of religion in fact only one offering that at once presents us with God who is no sort of extension or projection of ourselves or other creatures, who has no place for "great green-eyed Pasht" or the male or female divinities projected by our lusts or insecurities, and yet does not abandon us in finitude. The protagonist of the Gospels is, as Chalcedon has it, always "one and the same" actor, one and the same subject, whether doing God-things like sanctifying creatures or human-things like suffering pain and death. Where he is, God is very much available among us. And just so, the difference of God and creature is made inescapable, for no one but God could suffer as does Jesus and no one but a creature could be glorified as he is. The preaching and liturgical practice and pastoral practice that will liberate from superstition is preaching and liturgy and counseling inspired and normed by the strictest Cyrillean christological orthodoxy.

We must also take into account our distinction between the two *logoi* that post-Christianity offers the old gods or their simulacra when they return. Considering first the situation in which superstition is given grammar and coherence by the expectation of nothingness, we note a clear if peculiar apologetic opportunity.

Sherlock Holmes famously said that when you eliminate possibilities until finally only one is left, that is the solution no matter how improbable. That a first-century Palestinian Jew, precisely as the individual person he is, should be the structuring point of the universe, would not be the first guess of minds schooled by the great Greek thinkers. But the long experiment of Western civilization has eliminated all the mediating possibilities, reducing them to superstition. We have left just the two: waiting for nothingness or waiting for Jesus. And since nihilism is demonstrably not an intelligible thought, waiting for Jesus is the rational choice.

Insofar as the superstition we face is instead given grammar and coherence by abstracted Christianity, it must be our apologetic and liturgical and homiletical task to reclaim such abstractions as "love" and "peace" and "empowerment" and so forth to their proper meaning as mere slogans for the concrete person of the risen Christ. A great deal of our preaching and teaching is exactly backwards. So, for example, the preacher will say that what a text from one of the Gospels, about a miracle or parable, "is really about is acceptance of people in all their diversity." A true sermon would go just the other way: "What our talk of acceptance and diversity etc. is really trying to get at is Jesus."

And there is an apologetic possibility here also. It is easy to show that the roster of slogans that make up abstracted Christianity is incoherent except as slogans about this person, this risen crucified male first-century Palestinian Jew. Can peace and justice really kiss each other? All experience says not; but Christians add, except as characterizations of what this man did and suffered and does.

Superstition is in Father Brown's phrase an "endless vista"; it is an indefinity of everything in general and nothing real. Faith is concentrated vision; it is particular and enabled only by the particular presented to it. The post-Christian West is endless vista, and the church — if it is to be any use at all — must concentrate ever more on its particular, on the man he was made and the he of whom this can be true.

Religion and Secularity in a Culture of Abstraction: On the Integrity of Space, Time, Matter, and Motion

DAVID L. SCHINDLER

I

Wendy Kaminer, in a 1996 article in *The New Republic*,[1] argues that the current problem regarding religion in America is not, as is often lamented, that we have too little of it, but that we have too much of it. While advocates of religiosity extol the moral habits that religion is supposed to instill in us, she says they need to pay more attention to the intellectual habits it discourages in us. Religion sanctifies bad thinking, preempting the inner dynamic of intelligence through arbitrary appeals to authority — scriptural or clerical or mystical — that issue in premature closure. What America needs, therefore, is not more religion but more secularism.

Now in fact I agree with Kaminer that there is a significant sense in which contemporary America has too much religion. But I also agree in a significant sense with those she criticizes, who insist on the contrary that contemporary America "suffer[s] from an excess of secularism." To put it another way: I believe with the "left" that American religiosity typically harbors an inadequate sense of and appreciation for the secu-

---

1. Wendy Kaminer, "The Last Taboo," *The New Republic* (October 14, 1996), pp. 24-28, 32.

lar; and I believe with the "right" that American secularity has wrongly emancipated itself from religion — has emancipated itself in ways that presuppose, however unconsciously, an inadequate sense of religion. How is it possible to hold both of these positions simultaneously?

In attempting to answer this question, we need first to take note of the profound, if ironic, sense in which the left and the right agree regarding religion in America, coincident with the disagreement signaled by Kaminer's article. For both sides apparently accept the polls indicating that "almost all Americans (95 percent) profess belief in god or some universal spirit," that "seventy-six percent imagine God as a heavenly father who actually pays attention to their prayers" (Kaminer, 24), and other such data. That this is so for "liberals" like Kaminer is a relatively straightforward matter: the data provide empirical support for her lament about the pervasiveness of religion.

For "conservatives" the matter is more complex. On the one hand, thinkers on the right are likewise often quick to appeal to such data, to confirm their judgment that America is a "nation with the soul of a church," and thus to decry the myth of a secularistic America. On the other hand, these same thinkers are equally quick to identify a growing relativism or indeed nihilism in contemporary culture, calling attention to widespread support for legalized abortion, gay marriage, and the like. Such thinkers, then, explain the apparent discrepancy between what they regard as an innate American religiosity and growing signs of secularism largely by "regionalizing" the phenomenon of secularism: restricting it, say, to the "knowledge elite," or to what they regard as the left-leaning "knowledge class," in contrast to the ordinary mass of Americans who, in the ways suggested by the polling data, persist in their religiosity. These thinkers, moreover, are inclined to conceive the secularism of this left-leaning knowledge class primarily as a sign of bad will: as a moral falling-away from what they regard as an originally structurally sound American religion.

It is just here that I wish to focus our discussion: in their interpretation of the polling data indicating widespread religiosity, neither the (so-called) secular left nor the (so-called) religious right in their prevalent forms notice the profound ways in which religion and secularism in America, in their original "logic," grow from the same soil.[2] On

2. Cf. the now "classical" argument of Will Herbert, in his *Protestant, Catholic, Jew* (Chicago: University of Chicago Press, 1983).

the contrary, however much they differ in other (important) respects, the left and the right both commonly assume that American religion — in its original and historically dominant forms, Protestant and Catholic — stands in fundamental opposition to contemporary secularism. Both sides assume that religion and secularism in America are essentially separate and discrete phenomena, such that where one is present the other is just so far absent, where one increases, the other just so far diminishes. They assume, in a word, that the division between religion and secularism is clean and fundamental.

My proposal is that the division between religion and secularism in America is not so clean and fundamental; that these phenomena are rather more like two different branches of the same tree or, to change the metaphor, like two quarreling siblings unaware that they are born of the same parents.

Let me stress that I do not mean by this to suggest that the polling data regarding religion in America are altogether insignificant, or that the religiosity indicated by these polls is insincere. Nor do I mean to suggest that the conflicts — what some term the "culture wars" — between the secular left and the religious right are not very real, that moral issues are not an important part of these conflicts, or that the two sides in the conflicts are worthy of equal and symmetrical criticism. My proposal is simply that there exists an original and indeed continuing coincidence between religion and secularism in America, and that, unless we understand the nature of this coincidence, we remain incapable of interpreting properly the polling data indicating religiosity, or of developing an adequate response in the face of our so-called "culture wars."

Thus my argument, as it concerns Christians, is that the problem of secularism in America begins in a significant sense within the (Protestant and Catholic) churches themselves and their theology and religious practices. To put it in its most radical and indeed what seem to me also most precise terms, the disappearance or indeed the death of God is a phenomenon occurring not only in the 5 percent of Americans who do not profess belief in God but also and more pertinently in the 95 percent who do. (Nietzsche's "diagnosis" holds not only for nineteenth-century Europe but also for nineteenth- and twentieth-century America.)

My general proposal, then, in light of the above, is that America's defective religiosity has largely set the terms for America's defective secularity — or secularism, and that the relation between these is mutual; and that we can therefore respond constructively to today's cultural situation as it concerns religion and secularity only by reconceiving both, *simultaneously*.

This article takes the form mostly of entering a series of qualifiers, followed by examples, intended to clarify the meaning of these assertions.

II

A statement by Wendell Berry, one of America's most thoughtful and imaginative writers, brings us immediately to the heart of the matter: "perhaps the great disaster of human history," he says, "is one that happened to or within religion: that is, the conceptual division between the holy and the world, the excerpting of the Creator from the creation."[3] "The churches . . . excerpt sanctity from the human economy and its work just as Cartesian science has excerpted it from the material creation. And it is easy to see the interdependence of these two desecrations: the desecration of nature would have been impossi-

---

3. "A Secular Pilgrimage," in *A Continuous Harmony: Essays Cultural and Agricultural* (New York: Harcourt Brace, 1972), pp. 3-35, at 6. This dualism "between Creator and creature," which unravels into a series of further dualisms — between "spirit and matter, religion and nature, religion and economy, worship and work, and so on" — "is the most destructive disease that afflicts us" ("Christianity and the Survival of Creation," in *Home Economics* [New York: North Point, 1987], p. 105). Although the religion Berry has most in mind here is a Puritan Protestantism, modern Catholicism has had its own version of the dualisms to which he refers. It suffices to note the work of Henri de Lubac, and recall the great resistance that greeted de Lubac's attempts to recover the social-cosmic dimension of Catholicism and of the Eucharist (in *Catholicisme* and *Corpus Mysticum*, for example), and to retrieve a more organic and concrete form of the God/world relation (in his work on grace and nature in *Surnaturel* and *Le Mystère du Surnaturel*, for example). De Lubac's concern, not unlike that of Berry, was to draw attention again to what had been largely lost from view in the modern era, namely, God's original and intrinsic, if wholly unearned and unanticipated, invitation to the world to share in his own life and hence holiness. De Lubac understood this invitation in terms of the sacramental mediation of the church in a way that Berry does not address. The point is simply that de Lubac and Berry are, notwithstanding, in profound agreement regarding the need for Christianity to reject the dualism that undergirds a conception of salvation as individualistic and, as it were, world-less. For an overview of the problematic here as it concerns de Lubac, see my "Introduction to the 1998 Edition," Henri de Lubac, *The Mystery of the Supernatural* (New York: Crossroad/Herder and Herder, 1998).

CREATOR   SPIRIT   RELIGION   RELIGION   WORSHIP
CREATION   MATTER   NATURE   ECONOMY   WORK

ble without the desecration of work, and vice versa."[4] In a word, the excerpting of the Creator from his creation prevents creation — the world — from being understood as a destined dwelling place for holiness.

What I wish to propose, in light of this statement by Berry, is that there is an intrinsic connection between a religion originally reduced by its dualistic reading of the relation between God and the secular and a secularity that is thereby itself originally reduced by virtue of the same dualism. This original "secularizing"-through-dualistic-reduction of the secular remains hidden and appears harmless so long as relation to God continues to be — arbitrarily — added to the secular, an addition that has been readily forthcoming throughout most of America's history. Today, however, this "secularizing" reduction of the secular has taken a more overt and aggressive form, turning more explicitly *against* religion. My point is that this should really come as no surprise: a secularity that has been given its original meaning in abstraction from God already and in principle conceives relation to God as an arbitrary addition to itself. It is a small logical step to construe this arbitrary addition, over time, as an imposition from without: as something to be kept at a distance or indeed removed altogether from the secular, precisely to safeguard secularity's original integrity *as secular*.[5] Thus is an anti-religious hostility born from the heart of an original secularizing dualism for which religion itself (also) bears responsibility.

At any rate, that is what I wish to propose: the oppositions in today's dialectic in America between religion and secularism, or religionists and secularists, are oppositions originating from different sides of the coin of the same theological-ontological dualism identified by Berry. However significant their differences in assessing our current cultural situation — and these differences are significant — religionists and secularists alike begin by accepting, albeit from different directions and however tacitly and unwittingly, the separation, or

---

4. "God and Country," in *What Are People For?* (New York: North Point, 1990), pp. 96-97.

5. Again, it should be stressed that religionists intended this separation to be itself an expression of religious devotion, one that protected the gratuitousness of God's creation and guaranteed God's transcendence. The problem is that they construed this rightful gratuitousness and transcendence of God — of the God of Revelation — in terms of a "superadded" relation that presupposed an original extrinsicism.

extrinsic relation, between God and the *saeculum* — the world or cosmos — that is a hallmark of American religion's (Protestant and Catholic) original, and dominant, self-understanding.

III

Of course, there is much about the claim that American religion begins in an original separation between God and the world that strikes one as immediately counterintuitive, and thus we need to qualify. Surely the evidence of history, confirmed again in today's polls, suggests that Americans are inveterately pious: from the beginning until today they have been abundantly inclined to relate events in the world to God's will or providence. In any case, it would seem odd indeed to try to convict the Puritans (for example) of not doing this. In my discussion of dualism above, I used the term "abstraction" — referring to an original abstraction of secularity from relation to God — but this seems only to make my claim less tenable: surely the Puritans, as well as present-day Christians, do not intend to abstract the things they do in this world from the provident will of God.

Here, then, is the needed and crucial qualifier. The dualism we are alleging is twofold: it consists in an extrinsic relation between the will or volition, on the one hand, and intelligence or cognitive order, on the other, in our original engagement with God and the world; and it consists at the same time in an extrinsic relation between God and the world, or again in a false abstraction from God in our original understanding of the world. This abstraction is not from a simply transcendent monopolar God but from the transcendent-immanent trinitarian God hypostatically united to man in Jesus Christ. The abstraction between will and cognitive order that we are calling false, in other words, itself presupposes a double extrinsicism: between the God of natural reason and the God of supernatural faith, and hence between the orders of reason (nature) and revelation (supernature).

The abstraction of the world or secularity from God to which I have referred is therefore a matter not primarily of volition but of intelligent-cosmic order. The will (in the form of supernatural faith) maintains (intends to maintain) real relation to God as it engages the world, even as the ("natural") intelligence engages that same world in terms of an order that has been first abstracted from the trinitarian

God incarnate in Jesus Christ, and consequently from a creation made in the image of this trinitarian God and destined already in its constitutive created structure to share in God's trinitarian love and beauty, in and through Jesus Christ (Col. 1:15-18).[6] We might say that Christians have been careful watchdogs of morality and inner-churchly piety even as they have largely given away the orders of space, time, matter, and motion — and indeed the entire realm of the body and bodiliness, and of the artifacts and institutions in and through which space, time, matter, and motion become human culture. The dualism I am alleging in America, in a word, may be described as an originally moralized and "voluntarized" *religiosity* coincident with an originally "mechanized" cosmic and even divine *order*. The words of theologian Robert Jenson are apt here: "Our 'liberalism' and our 'conservatism' are but the atheist and superstitious branches of the same capitulation before a dead [read: mechanistic] universe."[7]

Thus, regarding Americans' proclivity for relating their secular or "worldly" lives to God: the giving away of the orders of space and time and matter and motion to which I refer does not mean that Christians do not still see these realities as subject to a proper *use:* see them, that is, as instruments in and through which the will of God is to be faithfully executed. The relevant point, rather, is that this appeal to a (putative) moral or faithful *use* of things, in its conventional understanding, typically begs the set of questions we mean to be raising. It presupposes and reinforces just the voluntaristic piety we are insisting is the nub of the issue. A cosmos originally understood as "neutral" or "dead" stuff, hence as essentially blind and dumb until appropriated as an instrument of moral or pious choices, indicates a cosmos that is originally indifferent to God. And such a cosmos itself already and as a matter of principle maneuvers piety — the pious use of the cosmos — into what now becomes mostly a moralistic — because precisely arbitrary — imposition on the cosmos.[8] The point, in short, is

---

6. Cf. fn. 3 regarding de Lubac and the sacramental mediation of the church.

7. Robert Jenson, *America's Theologian* (New York: Oxford University Press, 1988), p. 34.

8. Cf. here the statement of Luigi Giussani: Genuine morality occurs when "one's behavior flows from the dynamism intrinsic to the event to which it belongs"; moralism on the contrary is "an arbitrary and pretentious selection of affirmations among which the choices most publicized by power will dominate" ("Religious Awareness in Modern Man," *Communio* 25 [Spring, 1998]: 132 and *passim*). The point is that an authentic mo-

that an appeal to the moral or pious use of the world, as conventionally understood in America, expresses just the defective conception of both holiness and secularity that, in the way indicated by Berry, lies at the root of current difficulties.

Here we can see the response also to the view which assumes that the rationalized and mechanized world or cosmos is harmless — because neutral — except at those critical junctures where this world challenges religion or morality on specific issues and in explicit ways (for example, in the matter of abortion, or the cloning of human beings, or the bodily resurrection of Jesus Christ, and so on). But such a view fails to notice that the rationalized and mechanized world itself already presupposes American religion's positivistic self-understanding. And, again, it is just this self-understanding that reinforces the secular climate within which morality and religion are now perceived as arbitrary additions to the inner "logic" of the secular world's own order — and experienced just so far as mostly intrusions upon that order.

Thus, to return to our opening remarks: why should we be surprised if Americans today are disposed increasingly to dismiss religion with its attendant morality as arbitrary and irrelevant, when religion in its dominant American-Christian forms has defined *itself* as irrelevant: irrelevant, that is, to the world the integration of whose *secular order* religion has conceded already to have occurred on that order's own terms, in abstraction from constitutive (albeit, to be sure, gratuitous) relation to the trinitarian God? Why should we be surprised if Americans increasingly experience Christianity as alien to their secular experience, when their Christianity has already defined *itself* as alien to secular experience — to experience *in its original integrity as secular?* That is my question.

America's secular culture, in a word, is today largely in the process of turning inside out America's own religious self-understanding.

---

rality cannot flow from a cosmos that is originally dumb and blind, hence not open in its intrinsic structure to the destiny intended in authentic moral choices. For the full meaning and consequences of these suggestions, see the discussion below, especially that concerning Romano Guardini. Cf. also my "Is Truth Ugly? Moralism and the Convertibility of Being and Love," *Communio* 27 (Winter, 2000): 701-28.

IV

These are to be sure strong words. Let me now back up and clarify the nature and key elements of the argument, which I will then illustrate in terms of the contemporary situation particularly as discussed in my own — Roman Catholic — tradition.

Earlier I introduced what may seem to some an extreme claim regarding the disappearance of God also among the 95 percent of Americans who profess belief in God, and not only among the 5 percent who are explicit in their denial of God's existence. I have qualified that claim to signify the disappearance of God primarily, not in the moral will or religious intentions of Christians in America, but in Christians' sense of the *order of things*, or the *intelligent ordering of things, in the cosmos*. And I have suggested that this disappearance is brought about by an abstraction from God in one's original understanding of the cosmos, resulting in an original "rationalizing" and "mechanizing" of the cosmos. My argument, then, hinges decisively on the nature of a distinction: between will and intelligence and between God and the world — or between the monotheistic God of "natural" reason and the trinitarian God of faith — in our original understanding of the world. It may, however, still seem a mouthful — not to say a trifle "intellectualist" — to hang the death of God and an entire cultural crisis on the nature of a distinction. Let me therefore first describe briefly how I understand the historical origin of what I am suggesting is a false (because dualistic) distinction, and how, in this light, I am understanding the nature of a distinction, as it pertains to the matters at hand.

(1) Theologian Hans Urs von Balthasar locates the origin of the West's dualistic religious sense in what he terms the split between theology and sanctity, or again between theology and "Christian life."[9] Up until after the time of the great Scholastics, the great saints, he says, were, mostly, great theologians. "Their . . . lives reproduced the fullness of the Church's teaching, and their teaching the fullness of the Church's life" (181). The unity of knowledge and life was the canon of truth for these thinkers. "But as theology increasingly took

---

9. "Theology and Sanctity," in *The Word Became Flesh* (San Francisco: Ignatius Press, 1989), pp. 181-209 ("Theologie und Heiligkeit," in *Verbum Caro* [Einsiedeln: Johannes Verlag, 1960], pp. 195-225).

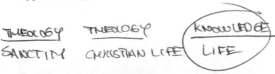

on a 'scholastic' form, through the advent of Aristotelianism, the
naïve unity hitherto accepted was gravely shaken" (184). "Philosophy
began to emerge as a discipline alongside theology, with its own concept of philosophical truth" (185). It was emphatically not the case for
Balthasar that this concept of truth did not have a certain — important — legitimacy. The point was rather that philosophy as it developed tended to focus one-sidedly on truth conceived in abstraction
from its concrete and ultimately personal-divine origin. The issue, in
other words, was not whether a distinction between philosophical
truth and theological truth was necessary — Balthasar is unequivocal
that it is — but how it was to be understood.[10] Thus, as he puts it:

> The intimate connection was seen, and indeed emphasized, between
> the true and the good as the transcendental properties of the one be-
> ing, but it was looked at more from the human standpoint, in the mu-
> tual presupposition of intellect and will . . . , than in their objective
> mutual inclusion. . . . Philosophy, as a doctrine of natural being and
> excluding revelation, could not know that the highest mode of inter-
> preting that philosophical definition of truth must be a trinitarian
> one, corresponding to the passages on truth in St. John . . . (185).

Balthasar says that it took the greatness of a Bonaventure or a Thomas
"to irradiate and transfigure [this] self-subsisting science of nature,
raising it to the plane of the sacred, and so to impart to the secular sciences a real Christian ethos, one affecting the whole outlook of the
scientific endeavor" (186). The difficulties began to emerge when the

> philosophical propaedeutic [in the guise, for example, of a natural
> theology antecedent to biblical theology] came to be considered a
> fixed and unalterable basis, whose concepts, without the necessary
> transposition, were used as norms and criteria of the content of faith,
> and therefore set in judgment over it. Teachers behaved as though
> man knew from the outset, before he had been given revelation, knew
> with some sort of finality what truth, goodness, being, light, love and

---

10. See, for example, Balthasar's positive comments regarding the influence of
Aristotelianism in the emergence of the rightful independence of the modern sciences
of nature and mind, and the gain in enormous clarity and insight from this development: "Theology and Sanctity," pp. 184-85. For Balthasar's view regarding the distinct,
positive contribution of Scholasticism, cf., inter alia, his "Patristics, Scholastics, and
Ourselves," *Communio* 24 (Summer, 1997): 347-96.

faith were. It was as though divine revelation on these realities had to accommodate itself to these fixed philosophical concepts of philosophy and their content, before going on to their application in theology (186).

Thus there emerged a double movement: a separation of philosophy from theology, coincident with what then became the pressure to reduce theological truth to philosophical truth — especially as students were eventually required to familiarize themselves with the concepts of philosophy and their content, before going on to apply these concepts in theology (180).[11]

The epoch following Bonaventure and Thomas, says Balthasar, saw the completion of the split between theology and spirituality. "Spiritual men were turned away from a theology which was overlaid with secular philosophy — with the result that alongside dogmatic theology, meaning always the central science which consists in the exposition of revealed truth, there came into being a new science of the 'Christian life,' one derived from the mysticism of the Middle Ages and achieving independence in the *devotio moderna*" (187).[12]

There are to be sure enormously complex developments distilled here.[13] (It would be interesting, for example, to trace, in light of the history indicated, the origins of the explicit nature-supernature dualism within Catholic theology in the fifteenth and sixteenth centuries; of the Reformation; and indeed of the methods and contents of modern science.) My purpose in offering this brief historical sketch is simply to indicate the sense in which the dualistic distinction with which I have been concerned — between will and intelligence, or again be-

---

11. It should be pointed out here that it is not the case for Balthasar that philosophy does not, or may not, retain a relative priority over theology, or that philosophy may never precede theology. The issue, rather, turns on whether and in what sense philosophy, if and insofar as it is studied prior to theology, nonetheless remains intrinsically open to revelation.

12. See, for example, the discussion by Balthasar in *The Glory of the Lord*, vol. 5: *The Realm of Metaphysics in the Modern Age* (San Francisco: Ignatius Press, 1991), pp. 9-47. Cf. also in this connection Graham Ward, "Introduction, or, A Guide to Theological Thinking in Cyberspace," in *The Postmodern God* (Oxford: Blackwell, 1997), pp. xv-xlvii, esp. at xxiii-xxiv.

13. See, for example, Michael Buckley's *At the Origins of Modern Atheism* (New Haven: Yale University Press, 1987); and my discussion of this book in "The Catholic Academy and the Order of Intelligence: The Dying of the Light?" *Communio* 26 (Winter, 1999): 722-45, at 730-33.

tween voluntaristic religiosity and mechanistic secular order — has an "existential" origin and meaning. This distinction, in other words, in its original historical form represents a failure on the part of Christians *to carry through in their lives the integration of all aspects of being — here especially the mind and intelligent order — in terms of the relation to God that is the heart of the call to holiness.* What we have been describing in conceptual terms as a dualistic distinction first appeared not outside of but within experience, precisely as the "logic" of that experience: Christians' relation to God, existentially, became increasingly voluntaristic in nature, even as Christians' understanding of the order of the cosmos became increasingly abstract.[14] The logic of that experience, in sum, consisted in the double abstraction to which we have referred: of intelligent order both from the God of revelation and from will and affectivity. Balthasar identifies this abstraction in terms of a displacement of the centrality of glory in our understanding of God and of beauty in our understanding of the secular order of things. We will return to this important question of beauty later. First, two comments about the nature of the distinction about which I am arguing, in light of Balthasar's overview.

(2) (a) Returning to the question of American culture, when I say that America's current problems regarding religion and secularism turn decisively on the nature of a distinction, I do not refer in the first instance to a conceptual distinction consciously and explicitly formulated as such, an idea from which our current cultural problems are supposed then to have deductively unraveled. It is not the case that there was first an idea which then produced an experience, but rather that the original (and dominant) American experience itself contained, as one of its distinct but not exhaustive features, an intelligent *order* or *ordering*: a "logic." To be sure, this logic has, from the beginning and all along the way, also been given explicit theological formulation, which in turn has reinforced and guided the original experience. The point is that the logic — the nature of the distinction — upon which I take our religious-cultural situation so decisively to hang is a matter first and fundamentally of a logic *implicit in a way of life.*

The consequences of this organic relation of logic and way of life, then, are two. Insofar as the logic is always already inside the experience, it cannot but always influence and direct that experience. At the

14. Cf. Buckley, *At the Origins of Modern Atheism.*   AFFECTIVITY

VOLUNTARISTIC RELIGIOSITY -HEART / WILL

MECHANISTIC SECULAR ORDER -HEAD / INTELLIGENCE

same time, insofar as this logic is itself but one element of the total experience — because, as Balthasar's historical analysis indicates, the total experience includes not only intelligence but also will and affectivity and the like — this logic never wholly determines the content or direction of the experience, but is in fact partially determined *by* this experience.

What my argument is asserting, in short, is that the logic of dualism in crucial ways shapes even as it does not exhaustively account for today's cultural situation. It represents merely the logic of the situation. What I am urging in response, therefore, is an entire way of life, but one *that essentially includes a new and distinct logic.*

(2)(b) But there is a more radical question regarding whether our insistence on the importance of the nature of a distinction for our cultural situation, even with the foregoing qualification, is still not too "academic" or "intellectualist." To put it in its most trenchant form: Does my argument mean to imply that this situation can be accounted for without recourse to the reality of sin?

I raise this question to make clear that of course I have no intention of attenuating the reality of sin as a source, indeed, the most fundamental source, of our current troubles. My argument, rather, merely implies a challenge to the moralistic-voluntaristic reduction of sin that is the obverse of what I have identified as the moralistic-voluntaristic piety of Americans. My argument, in other words, implies an expansion of the notion of sin, along the lines indicated in what Pope John Paul II calls sin's structural dimension. Perhaps the best definition of what he means by this is given in his encyclical *Dominum et vivificantem:*

> Unfortunately, the resistance to the Holy Spirit which Saint Paul emphasizes in the *interior and subjective dimension* as tension, struggle and rebellion taking place in the human heart finds in every period of history and especially in the modern era its *external dimension,* which takes concrete form as the content of culture and civilization, *as a philosophical system, an ideology, a programme* for action and for the shaping of human behavior (56).

And again in *Sollicitudo Rei Socialis:*

> Sin and structures of sin are categories which are seldom applied to the situation of the contemporary world. However, one cannot easily

gain a profound understanding of the reality that confronts us unless we give a name to the root of the evils which afflict us (36).

Thus sin bears not only a subjective but also an external or "objective" dimension: it takes the form of an idea or a philosophy informing a program or institution or indeed civilization. To be sure, as the pope insists elsewhere, sin in this "structural" sense is always finally personal — that is, originates finally in someone's personal, or subjective, act. The point is simply that this subjective (or moral or voluntary) dimension of sin itself extends "beyond" subjectivity, expressing itself in an objectively disordered meaning. Personal sin has not only a voluntary or subjective but also a cognitive or objective dimension, an objective dimension which is social, extending into, and embodied in and informing, social-political-cultural institutions. (Or, in other words, as we indicated above, every experience contains a distinct "logos" or claim about objective order that makes the experience at once personal and social.)

The burden of my argument, therefore, in light of the pope's analysis, is not that America's religious-cultural problems have nothing to do with sin in the subjective sense — which would be ludicrous — but that these problems have to do in a particularly significant way with the structural-objective sin that reaches beyond even as it remains intrinsically connected with "subjective" sin. If my argument does not emphasize the moral, or subjectively sinful, dimension of America's problems, this is only because this dimension is hardly unique to Americans: presumably Americans' lives are a mixture of moral viciousness and moral virtue much like the lives of all people in the infralapsarian period. What I wish to emphasize is that what is most peculiar about America is the way in which its religion — and its liberal tradition — have from the beginning dissociated questions of will and morality from questions of intelligence and cosmic-ontological order; the way in which, accordingly, America's moralized-voluntarized religion has persisted coincident with a secularized cosmic-intelligent order.

The further crucial point, as already hinted, is that America's distinctive piety, in presupposing as it does a moralized-voluntarized notion of sin, thereby renders invisible what we, following John Paul II, have identified as the objective, or structural or intellectual, dimension of sin. That is, the peculiar nature of American religion is that it

MORALIZED/VOLUNTARIZED

SECULAR COSMIC-INTELLIGENT ORDER

46   DAVID L. SCHINDLER

renders sin invisible precisely as a matter (also) of distinctly *cognitive dis-order*. But the point is that it is sin in just this cognitive or structural sense that needs above all now to be brought into relief, as the condition *sine qua non* for a proper understanding of America's current cultural situation.

But it is time now to illustrate the content of my argument directly in terms of this cultural situation. We have suggested that America's abstraction of intelligent order from will and affectivity and from the trinitarian God expresses and generates reduced notions of space, time, matter, and motion — a reduction that is properly termed at once a fragmentation and a secularization.[15] And we have suggested further that these fragmented and secularized notions of cosmic order in fact constitute "structural sin." What does all of this mean concretely?

V

I will respond primarily in terms of the project of Anglo-American modernity, as engaged especially by my own — Roman Catholic — tradition. The concern, in light of the foregoing argument, is to identify how and where the dead cosmos — the mechanistic, hence dumb and blind, order of space and time and matter and motion that make up nature and indeed culture — manifests itself in this tradition.

(1) To do this, we can look at the reading of American institutions — political, economic, academic — prevalent among Catholics in recent decades, which indeed has been justified increasingly in terms of Vatican II and in the name of the present pontificate. For example, in the political realm, we have John Courtney Murray's "articles of peace" reading of the First Amendment, which maintains that America's official political institution (the state) is, as such, empty of any notion of

15. Cf. here the pertinent comment of Graham Ward in his introduction to *The Postmodern God*, relative to the problem of what may be termed "postmodernity," that "modernism is linked to specific conceptions of space, time, and substance, and that postmodernism explodes the myths and ideologies constructing these conceptions" (p. xvii). And again: "If we wish to apprehend the postmodern God," he says, "we have . . . to investigate the project of modernity with reference to the shapes it gave to time, space, and bodies. For these shapes portrayed the face of modernity's god — the god whom Nietzsche (following a suggestion by Hegel) pronounced dead" (p. xvii).

human destiny — until members of society, in the course of a free market exchange of ideas, put some such notions there. In the economic realm, we have the (so-called neoconservative) disciples of Murray arguing, in the name of John Paul II's *Centesimus Annus,* that that encyclical's distinction between culture and economics should be read in the same Murrayite, "articles of peace," vein: insisting that the economic system as such is empty of any theology or anthropology, and that religious or moral evaluations of that system turn first on how the system is used or on the ends to which it is instrumentalized. Finally, in the realm of the academy, and again in a Murrayite spirit, prominent American Catholic educators have claimed, in accord with the Land O' Lakes statement and indeed also in the name of Vatican II, that the Catholic university is substantially a university and only adjectivally Catholic. That is, the modern university — in its original definition as a university — indicates first an order of critical-disciplinary methods, procedures, and categories (university as a noun), to which a Catholic or Buddhist or Islamic or Jewish worldview or ethics is to be added (adjectival qualification). The pertinent point, once again, is that the order of the university as such is conceived to be originally empty of, hence neutral toward, any definite notion of the ontological destiny of man and cosmos.

My simple suggestion is that all of these readings of the world as ordered into institutions share a common view of order as first and most basically dumb and blind, which is to say, mechanistic. To put it another way, the distinction between "institution" and "ideology" as accepted here by Catholic thinkers, which Joseph Komonchak among others has affirmed — rightly in my opinion — as a hallmark feature of Anglo-American liberalism,[16] in fact presupposes and reinforces just the dualism of moralism and voluntarism on the one hand and mechanism on the other that I have insisted is the bane of American culture. More precisely, the liberal distinction between institution and ideology subscribed to by Catholics, now in the name of the Second Vatican Council and the pontificate of John Paul II, expresses exactly the reduced sense of both God and secularity implied

16. See Joseph Komonchak, "Vatican II and the Encounter Between Catholicism and Liberalism," in *Catholicism and Liberalism: Contributions to American Public Philosophy,* ed. R. Bruce Douglass and David Hollenbach (Cambridge: Cambridge University Press, 1994), pp. 76-99.

by the positivistic sense of religion lying at the root of our present difficulties.

We have first the empty mechanisms of institutions whose order is dead, and which are then to be instrumentalized in and through what can now only be arbitrarily (i.e., voluntaristically) introduced religious-anthropological-ontological substance. In the parlance of today, the problem identified here as mechanism can alternatively be termed the problem of "proceduralism," in accord with which appeals to the formal mechanisms of the institution always arrive in advance of any substantive ideology, thereby already making that ideology into what is, from the perspective of the order of the institution as such, an arbitrary and hence unnecessary addition.

Let me be clear: the Catholic thinkers in question here all insist that the three respective institutions function properly only when guided by the substance of an adequate anthropology, in the form, for example, of the practice of natural law or of natural or civic virtue. My argument bears rather on the lateness of this addition as they conceive it. It bears precisely on the nature of a distinction — here between the order of the institution as such and the "ideology" or destiny to which it is put in service.

The main point, then, is that the addition of ideological substance as conceived by these Catholic thinkers is mediated by a modern — liberal — sense of distinction that itself already and as a matter of principle fragments the sense of distinction indicated by Catholicism.

That this is so can be illustrated briefly, for example, in terms of the difference between Aquinas and Descartes in their respective understandings of the order of the body. Both thinkers distinguish between soul (or human meaning: "psychics") and body (physical matter: "physics"). But Aquinas, unlike Descartes, does so all the while presuming an anterior unity between the two: with the crucially important consequence that the human meaning is not arbitrarily and just so far mechanically added to the body, nor is the original body sheer — which is to say morally and anthropologically empty — mechanism. Aquinas gives us an original body as organism, a body whose very physical order as body is always already related to, and hence far also "images," spiritual meaning.[17] And this is quite unlike

---

17. Pope John Paul II's notion of "nuptial body" is important for the discussion here, but how and why this is so must be shown elsewhere.

Descartes, who gives us an original body as machine, a set of dumb and blind procedures to which spiritual meaning is always yet to be added, instrumentally and arbitrarily, from outside. The point is that spirit and body both become profoundly different by virtue of how they are originally distinguished relative to one another: an intrinsic relation between the two yielding an organic space and time and matter (Aquinas), an extrinsic relation yielding a mechanistic space and time and matter (Descartes).

At any rate, my suggestion is simply that, in insisting that institutions, *in their original order as such*, are empty of spiritual-moral substance, the Catholic thinkers noted above are just so far committed, not to a neutral sense of (physical) order, but — however unwittingly — to a Cartesian (in contrast, for example, to a Thomistic) sense of order.

Again, let it be emphasized: the burden of my argument concerns not the simple denial but the late addition of anthropological-spiritual meaning. A Cartesian sense of worldly institutions implies a mechanized order juxtaposed to a human or indeed religious meaning, which meaning can now be introduced to that order only arbitrarily or voluntaristically. The liberal distinction between institution and ideology that many Catholics take to be sanctioned if not embraced by the Second Vatican Council is in fact an embodiment of the reduced sense of religion coincident with the reduced sense of the secular that bedevils contemporary American culture.

(2) But let me approach in another way the point urged here, drawing on a perceptive book by the late philosopher George Parkin Grant, *Technology and Justice*.[18]

In a chapter called "Thinking About Technology," Grant considers the extent to which "technology" has become "the pervasive mode of being in our political and social lives" (17). He reflects on a statement by a computer scientist that "the computer does not impose on us the ways it should be used" (19). This claim and the warrant offered for it, Grant says, are familiar to us: computers "are instruments, made by human skill for the purpose of achieving certain human goals. They are neutral instruments in the sense that the morality of the goals for which they are used is determined from outside them" (20).

Grant's argument is that this claim presupposes the "prevalent

18. Notre Dame: University of Notre Dame Press, 1986.

'liberal' view of the modern situation" — which, he says, "is so rooted in us that it seems to be common sense itself, even rationality itself. We have certain technological capacities; it is up to us to use those capacities for decent human purposes" (20-21). Indeed, he insists that such a claim asserts nothing less than "the essence of the modern view, which is that human ability freely determines what happens" (31).[19]

Against this claim regarding the computer as neutral instrument, Grant indicates the ways in which the computer embodies a certain conception of knowledge, an implied view of the relation between subject(ivity) and object(ivity), and between knowing and making, and a definite sense of the nature and place of "abstraction" and indeed information in human consciousness. The computer, further, carries an implied judgment about the nature of the other that is the object of knowledge, in a way that presupposes a particular view of the relation between knowledge and love and indeed of the nature of the other as beautiful (38ff.). Grant's point therefore is that the computer, far from being a neutral instrument, is in fact bound up finally with a whole conception of human destiny: the computer tends to homogenize its users in terms of that destiny. Regarding the claim that the computer does not impose itself upon us, then, Grant responds: "Common sense may tell us that the computer is an instrument, but it is an instrument from within the destiny which *does* 'impose' itself upon us, and therefore the computer *does* impose" (23). Grant summarizes thus:

> When we represent technology to ourselves as an array of neutral instruments, invented by human beings and under human control, we are expressing a kind of common sense, but it is a common sense from within the very technology we are attempting to represent. The novelness of our novelties is being minimized. . . . The coming to be of technology has required changes in what we think is good, what we think good is, how we conceive sanity and madness, justice and injustice, rationality and irrationality, beauty and ugliness.
>
>   . . . [The] changed conception of novelness . . . entails a change in the traditional account of an openness to the whole, and therefore a quite new content to the word "philosophy." A road or a sparrow, a child or the passing of time come to us through that destiny. To put

19. Cf. what I have called voluntarism.

the matter crudely: when we represent technology to ourselves through its own common sense, we think of ourselves as picking and choosing in a supermarket, rather than within the analogy of the package deal. We have bought a package deal of far more fundamental novelness than simply a set of instruments under our control. It is a destiny which enfolds us in its own conceptions of instrumentality, neutrality and purposiveness. It is in this sense that it has been truthfully said: technology is the ontology of our age (32).

What I wish to suggest, in light of this argument by Grant, is that the distinction between ideology and institution developed in the areas of politics, economics, and the academy by American Catholic thinkers in the ways indicated above, is a variant (analogous) expression of just this sense of ontology as technology: of order as mechanistic — dumb, blind, and neutral; and consequently of morality — which Grant discusses in terms of justice — as voluntaristic. This ontology represents, in short, what seems to me American Catholicism's distinctive contribution to secularism, to the secularized order characteristic of the increasingly globalized Anglo-liberal culture.

VI

But it is time now to attempt a summary of the positive import of our proposal. If I have interpreted matters accurately, what is most fundamentally at issue in our current religious-cultural situation is the nature of the cosmos in its creatureliness. At issue is the integrity of creation, in its constitutive relation to God. I have suggested that American religion characteristically fragments that integrity, through an abstraction of the mind or intelligent order or truth, from the concrete trinitarian God of revelation and from the will and the good. The result is a defective sense of religion, but also a defective sense of the secular. What I wish now to propose is that this defective sense of both religion and the secular can be identified best in terms of the displacement of beauty, for reasons already indicated briefly in our references to Balthasar and Grant. I wish to conclude by bringing into relief the intrinsic link between religion and beauty, that is, in its implications for an integrated view of secularity — of cosmos and culture.

I turn to two texts for assistance. The first is drawn from Grant's argument regarding the paradigm of knowledge he takes to be implied in the development of modern technology and in the liberal academic institutions characteristic of our technological age. Grant suggests that this paradigm turns on what is meant by objective knowledge and hence on the nature of the world as object.[20] He discusses this in terms of the meaning of faith, whose definition he takes from Simone Weil: "Faith is the experience that the intelligence is enlightened by love" (38). Grant says that this statement implies that "love is consent to the fact that there is authentic otherness" (38). That is, we love otherness (39); and we do so because and insofar as we perceive the other to be beautiful.

Thus for Grant the fundamental claim implied in Christian faith is the link between intelligent order and love. And beauty is the proper name for this link or integration. The modern world, insofar as it would be understood in light of faith, needs above all to (re-)center objective knowledge, which is to say, the world as object, the world in its objective order and meaning, in the beautiful. Those who would, in light of faith, have an adequate notion of secularity must just so far overcome the disjunction between the intelligent order or the truth of things and beauty — a disjunction summed up sharply in Nietzsche's dictum that "truth is ugly" (66).

To see the radical and comprehensive meaning of this assertion, in light of the integrated view of creation that is needed, we turn finally to another text, from Romano Guardini. "In the experience of a great love," he says, "all that happens becomes an event inside that love."[21] This statement is to be viewed first of all in terms of the revelation of God himself. That is, the whole of creation, everything in the cosmos, is an "experience" of God's great love; and the whole of creation thereby becomes an event inside that love. It follows that the world, and everything in the world — its space, its time, its matter, and its motion, every aspect of the order of cosmic being and activity — is first and most basically a gift. The world reflects not only the will but the mind of God (of the trinitarian God of love whose *logos* is revealed in Jesus Christ): the world reflects not only God's loving *will* but God's loving *order*.

Consider, for example, how even the material elements of the

20. Grant, *Technology and Justice*, pp. 36-37.
21. Cited by Giussani, "Religious Awareness in Modern Man," p. 137.

food prepared by the mother for her children take on the character of gift: that is, they are not only neutral instruments of her loving will. On the contrary, her love enters into the very space and time and matter and motion in and through which she prepares the food. These are no longer neutral instruments — blind and dumb instrument manipulated from outside by her will. On the contrary, these — this time and space and matter and motion — now become the very form of her love. Which is to say, these so-called instruments become intrinsic features — an intrinsic part — of the event of her love: they reveal, *by virtue of their own order now transformed by love,* the very face and figure of the mother.

What I am proposing is that this holds true, by way of analogy, for the entire cosmic order in its relation to God: every last bit of cosmic-cultural space, time, matter, and motion reveals — is destined to reveal — the face, the form, of God: the order of the event of God's great act of creative love.[22] Beauty, then, is the proper term for the *order* proper to what is *given* by God. Beauty, in short, is cosmic *order* understood as *gift.*

In sum: Nietzsche and Dostoëvsky, in their very different ways, are right about the crisis of modernity, even in America. Our crisis above all is a crisis of the death of God *simultaneous with* the death of beauty in the secular order of things.

With this, we return to our original set of questions regarding the prevalence in America of a voluntaristic religion and a mechanistic *saeculum.* The key to this dualism, we can now see more amply, is Christians' original detachment of the world's *giftedness from God* from the world's *order*: the uncoupling of the notions of *gift* and *order*, with a consequent moralizing of gift and formalizing of order. What is therefore demanded in response is twofold.

On the one hand, in terms of religion: what is needed is a deeper and more comprehensive sense of God now understood, in Jesus Christ and the church, to include the world, in a way that makes the world into the "sacrament" of God's presence.[23] And this sense of the world as the "sacrament" of God's presence demands, from within its

VOLUNTARISTIC RELIGION   GRACE   GIFT
MECHANISTIC SECULAR   NATURE   ORDER

22. Cf. fn. 3 above.

23. Cf. Alexander Schmemann, *For the Life of the World* (Crestwood, N.Y.: St. Vladimir's Press, 1998), p. 17.

own inner logic as religious, a re-centering of the whole of worldly logic, precisely as worldly-natural, in beauty.

On the other hand and at the same time, in terms of secularity: what is needed is a re-centering of the whole of the world, precisely in its own inner logic as natural and worldly, in beauty. And this re-centering of the world in beauty finally demands, by virtue of its own creaturely dynamism given gratuitously but constitutively by God, the world's transformation into the "sacrament" of God's presence — of God's glory.

These assertions, then, also indicate the method by which the re-newal of culture — or what is termed by Christians evangelization — is to be accomplished. The means whereby all of this is to be realized, simply, is the whole of one's life ordered by the love, friendship, and communion whose sacramental home is the church and the primary sense of which is aesthetic. This is so because, as Balthasar reminds us, "[t]he exchange of love that takes place within God is now open to the world in the form of an exchange between heaven and earth. . . ." In this exchange "the creature is not confronted with anything 'alien' but the innermost truth about the being and destiny of things and himself."[24] "This is what is meant by saying that the entire created universe has come into being in, through, and for the Word" (106).

RED

BLUE

YELLOW

CENTERING
GRACE INTO
NATURE (CREATION)

CENTERING
NATURE
IN TECHNOLOGY

CENTERING
NATURE (CREATION)
INTO GRACE

CENTERING
NATURE INTO
god

24. Citing Adrienne von Speyr, in *Theodrama*, vol. 5 (San Francisco: Ignatius Press, 1998), p. 105.

Postmodern Irony and Petronian Humanism: The New Challenges of Evangelism

R. R. RENO

We live in what we like to think of as a very sophisticated society. International commerce keeps the economy humming day and night. Silicon chips grease the wheels of calculation and communication. Medical centers are engaged in perpetual expansion as research facilities grow at a furious pace. Life gets more and more complicated. We can buy and sell Eurobonds on our cell phones while watching Monday Night Football at a Mexican theme sports bar owned by a partnership of German orthodontists. We can kill time after yet another flight cancellation by sipping latte and reading about treks from Lhasa to the Rongbuk Buddhist monastery at the base of Mount Everest. Our postmodern world is quite remarkable. There can be no doubt about it, the tectonic plates of culture are shifting.

If we care about evangelism, then surely we need to get our bearings in this strange, postmodern world. If we wish to preach and teach effectively, then we must be clear about where the sharp and double-edged sword of the gospel cuts into the spirit of the age. This is especially important because our own churches are awash with disorienting analysis. Some are eager to convince us that our sophisticated scientific culture just cannot accept the simplistic and mythological worldview of traditional Christianity. Others are certain that the new world of global communication makes us so aware of cultural and religious diversity that the traditional exclusivist claims of Christianity are untenable. Still others drink deeply at the well of literary theory and in an intoxicated reverie announce that old ideas of meaning and truth have been transcended. The essence of Scripture is not the person of Jesus Christ, but its openness to "difference." Most, however, offer a straightforward assessment: our postmodern world is so very, very complex that the traditional forms of Christian preaching and teaching must be updated and revised. I can hear the soundbite: "We need a message that speaks to the Internet Age."

These approaches to the no doubt new challenges of evangelism are wrongheaded. Each interprets the difficulties we face as the result of new facts. Somehow, scientific discovery or the global village of instant communication makes Christianity less plausible, as if the invention of the Internet poses sudden spiritual difficulties for Christian teaching. Somehow, new theoretical and philosophical fashions alter the landscape of consciousness, as if our minds are so much flotsam and jetsam pressed forward by the surging flood of cultural change. Somehow, the mere fact of social and technological complexity overwhelms the presumptive simplicity of old-fashioned Christianity, as if human beings had been ruminating animals without a care in the world before the advent of cellular phones and cable TV.

No, these approaches will not do. Instead, I propose another approach. The challenges facing Christian evangelism are not scientific; they are not technological; they are not philosophical or cultural in any theoretical or abstract sense. Instead, our challenges are moral and religious. The spirit of the age is, after all, *spiritual*. My goal, then, is to analyze these moral and spiritual challenges, for they, and not the undeniable changes on the surface of our society, shape the real task of evangelism. My thesis shall be that the confident humanism of modernity has given way to an anxious desire to escape moral demand and the pressure it puts on us to change.

I

To a great degree, we are told a story about modernity that emphasizes Promethean ambition. The high labors of freedom, the noble quest for equality, the rigors of critical thought are all championed as great achievements of the human spirit. In many cases, this story is accurate. Seminal modern figures were extraordinarily ambitious. For Rousseau, the human desire to integrate duty and sensibility was unquenchable, and for Kant, the light of conscience burned ever bright. Though unsentimental and often ruthless, both Hegel and Marx believed in the benevolent march of history toward a crowning humanism. John Stuart Mill and Bertrand Russell never underestimated the depths of human ignorance and irrationality, but both retained confidence in the integrity of reason and the triumphant power of argument. They differed from each other in many ways, but nonetheless, they held in common a confident hope. Our humanity, however understood, provides the sufficient basis for the highest good.

This confidence in human potency and potential defines modern humanism, and it creates a field of moral concerns that is shaped by two centers of gravity. The first is preoccupied with the creative potential of human agency. We have the spark of justice within, and the proper spiritual labor assigned to us is that of liberation. We must break down the constraining barriers that limit individuality and self-expression. Here, modernity is given over to the redemptive project of freedom. The other center of gravity is more cautious, but equally influential. This moral sensibility seeks to weigh evidence and avoid error. Quiet and uncoerced debate yields reliable truths, and our job is to resist the temptations of passionate excess and restrain foolhardy illusion. More skeptical and less speculative, this cautious humanism counsels moderation. We must be careful to tether our lives to secure and reliable anchors. We must build upon a firm and stable foundation.

The great American prophet, Ralph Waldo Emerson, penned epigrams that capture the ambition of the first aspect of modern humanism, its redemptive project, and his ambition certainly challenges Christian proclamation. Against the obedient discipline of *imitatio Christi*, Emerson claimed that "imitation is suicide." Against the self-condemning introspection of St. Augustine's repentant autobiography, Emerson substituted the affirmative principle, "trust thyself." Against the hierarchy of creature and Creator, Emerson insisted, "Nothing is sacred but the integrity of your own mind." Against the penitential imperative, Emerson interjected, "I do not wish to expiate, but to live." Against reliance upon a faith once delivered, Emerson stated, "The centuries are conspirators against the sanity and authority of the soul."[1] At every turn, Emerson is the brilliant strategist of the Promethean ambition of modernity. We must throw off the chains that bind, especially our psychic bondage to social and moral expectation, and then, in freedom, we can live according to the pure dictates of personal conscience.

Empiricists such as John Locke support the other side of modern humanism, its more cautious approach. For Locke, mental life is riven with prejudice and instability. The project of philosophy is to identify simple ideas that promise to remain stable, and on this basis, to rebuild intellectual life. In this effort, however, the true philosopher recognizes limits. As Locke writes, "It becomes the Modesty of Philosophy, not to pronounce Magisterially where we want that Evidence that can produce Knowledge."[2] Here, a skeptical temper moderates dogmatic tendencies. We should withhold assent to propositions unsupported by evidence. The goal, however, is not to propagate doubt for its own sake. Instead, for Locke and subsequent generations of empiricists, the purpose of the critical temper is to create social and psychic space for the incremental progress of scientific inquiry. Only if we release some of the pressure of traditional faith, only if we step back from the highly charged atmosphere of speculation and dogma, can we engage in the dispassionate and free exchange of ideas that leads to genuine and reliable intellectual results.[3]

Together, a zeal for freedom and a cool empiricism have nourished the modern spirit, and in both cases our humanity must take pride of place. For redemptive humanists such as Emerson, once liberated from the dead hand of dogma, our humanity is the creative and bountiful source of moral insight. For cautious humanists such as Locke, if we use critical doubt to reduce the demands of prejudice and social convention, then we can undertake the painstaking and slow process

1. All quotes from Emerson's essay, "Self-Reliance," *Essays: First and Second Series* (Cambridge, Mass.: Riverside Press, 1929), pp. 46-53.

2. *An Essay Concerning Human Understanding*, ed. Peter H. Nidditch (Oxford: Oxford University Press, 1975), p. 541.

3. For a classic statement of this cautious humanism, see Bertrand Russell's peroration on behalf of critical philosophy at the end of *The Problems of Philosophy*. For Russell, philosophy makes us sensible of the limitations of our knowledge, and as such, "it removes the somewhat arrogant dogmatism of those who have never travelled into the region of liberating doubt . . ." (Oxford University Press paperback reprint, 1959, p. 157). An impartial philosophical view allows us to transcend the "prison" and "strife" of merely private interest and personal prejudice. Just this openness permits the "free intellect" to attain higher and more universal knowledge.

of empirical inquiry. In both cases, human power displaces divine power as the source of hope. Emerson's hot passion and Locke's sweet reason guide us toward fulfillment. We are to break from traditional authority in order to release ourselves from hindering fetters, and in so doing, we accelerate the natural human push toward freedom and truth.

Not surprisingly, then, modern Christianity has sparred with modern humanism. After all, God comes first, not us. We must serve him in order to attain freedom. His truth shall judge the minds of men, and his word leads to all truth. Far from a hindering fetter, the authority of the gospel is the engine that drives us toward fulfillment. In spite of this obvious conflict, modern Christianity has not always opposed modern humanism, and for good reason. The antitheses are sufficiently pointed to suggest important common interests. The modern defense of individuality echoes the Christian confidence that God calls each of us by name. The new birth promised in baptism is not at all alien to Emerson's hope that we might disentangle ourselves from the cruel weight of the past. Justification by faith also turns us away from expiation and toward "life." Furthermore, like the close reasoning and rigorous argument endorsed by Locke, Christianity teaches doctrines as claims of truth, and not as nuggets of meaning. They possess public solidity and personal force. Against willfulness and inveterate human self-delusion, faith involves disciplining the mind to conform to the God-given facts. Like the empiricist, the theologian must serve that which is given.[4]

In both cases, whether ambitious or cautious, modern humanism shares with Christianity an interest in transformative power. Both are champions of change. For Emerson, freedom impels, for the restless divine spark of individuality always seeks full expression. He hopes for a time in which the radiance of individuality will illuminate the cosmos. For Locke, facts have force, and our minds receive the impress of their reality, and we should discipline ourselves to believe accordingly. Christianity preaches neither Emerso-

---

4. For an autobiographical account of the benefits for faith of the putatively atheistic approach of logical atomism, see Donald MacKinnon's essay, "Philosophy and Christology," found in *Borderlands of Theology* (New York: J. B. Lippincott, 1968), pp. 55-81. Mackinnon reports that engagement with philosophers such as Bertrand Russell brought him to see that knowing is a finding, not a fashioning, and that truth depended upon particularity, not an idea of the whole.

nian freedom nor Lockean empiricism, but the gospel also has potency to convert minds and change lives. The power of the cross
transforms sinner into saint. For this reason, modern humanism and
Christianity share a love of power and a hope for change, and given
this common love and common hope, many have sought to re-evan-
gelize modern western culture by reinterpreting modern humanism
and redirecting its account of the power of life toward the properly
Christian goal of putting God first. For apologists, the dynamics of
freedom and force of facts properly orbit around the power of the
cross, and Emerson and Locke, properly understood, advance the
cause of the gospel.

Maybe this attempt to conscript modern humanism to the task of
evangelism has been helpful. Maybe it has been a mistake. I have my
own views on the history of modern theology and its relationship to
modern humanism.[5] But I do not want to try to retrace the dialectical
gymnastics of someone like Paul Tillich, who thought that the redemptive promise of the gospel could be translated into Emersonian
phrases such as "Be all you can be." Such an exercise will not help us
orient ourselves in this postmodern context. Tillich and those modern
theologians like him who tried to ride the tiger of humanism are no
longer apt to the present. They no longer speak to the challenges of
preaching the gospel. The patrons of the Eternal Now seem to have
faded into the Already Past.

Why is someone like Tillich, the great patron of relevance, no
longer relevant? I think the answer is simple. The tenor of our age,
however humanistic in spirit, lacks the Promethean elements that
modern theology has long thought eternal. The Agent Orange of cultural critique has deforested our cultural imaginations, and we no
longer imagine ourselves to be heralds of freedom and truth. The
voices of condemnation and calls to repentance no longer challenge
our confident humanism; we hear such demands in the echo cham-
bers of therapeutic consciousness. After Freud, conscience cannot
stand against social authority, for the two are intertwined. Individuality remains a cherished ideal, but the multicultural agenda places
that ideal in the quicksand of race, class, and gender. For all our humanistic faith, we are not great believers in the intrinsic goodness

---

5. See my analysis in *Atonement and Personal Identity* (Trinity Press International,
forthcoming).

and integrity of human nature. We shrink from the harsh disciplines
that might shape our souls, even the humanistic disciplines of authenticity and rational inquiry. We need years of therapy in order to
overcome self-doubt, and even then, any consequent self-trust is
fragile. Still further, we worry about ideology and wring our hands
over the inevitable cultural limitations that undermine our quest for
knowledge. The boogieman of patriarchy is everywhere; everything
depends upon one's perspective. In all this, the effect is not
Emersonian ambition or Lockean confidence in reason. Pronouns are
changed, symbols are manipulated, critiques are undertaken, but almost always in the spirit of a new conformity that fears imprison-
ment without cherishing freedom.

In these and many other ways, the outlook of modernity has
shifted from ambition and confidence to fear and anxiety. The spirit
of the age is no longer self-expressive; it is self-protective. Whether
one is a Derridian, a disciple of Foucault, or a student of Heidegger,
the very potencies and powers that give human life dynamism and
drive are laden with danger. Allow me to list a few postmodern tru-
isms. Language is a vessel of power that seeks dominion. Truth
claims are tinged with imperial ambition. Technology alienates us
from life. Economic dynamism produces rapacious inequality. As a
consequence, the slogans of modernity may well endure; liberty,
equality, and fraternity may continue to be championed, but they are
so against a background of menace and not promise. Postmodern culture continues to put humanity first, but it does so in an atmosphere
tinged with fear.

Because postmodern culture is essentially defensive, the challenges of evangelism have changed, and the many modern theological
strategies of mediation are altogether beside the point. One need not
meet the rigorous demands of modern intellectual life when the present age is running in the opposite direction. One need not tailor the
gospel to fit the ambitions of freedom if the postmodern soul endeav-
ors to shrink to a point where it will no longer be noticed. But the demise of old challenges gives rise to new challenges. Postmodern humanism may not be Promethean, but it most certainly is not
Christian. In order to understand this new humanism, we need to ex-
amine its defensive posture. Two features are very much in evidence: a
fear of authority and a flight from truth. Both are integral to the
strange way in which postmodern culture seeks to serve humanity by

saving it from any and all power, by protecting us from the ambitions and demands that lead to change.[6]

II

The contemporary allergy to authority and flight from truth are certainly familiar to anyone who has sampled the air of American culture. Consider the slogan: "Celebrate diversity!" This platitude is so ubiquitous that it now seems self-evident. Some people are tall, others are short. It would be absurd to require all people to be the same height. Just as people are of different heights, we reason, so also do people have different spiritual sensibilities and needs. It would be absurd, then, to require them to hold the same beliefs or conform to the same moral rules. After all, only a violent attack upon the bodies of individuals would produce a world of people the same height. So also, we infer, enforced uniformity of belief and practice requires violent assaults upon conscience, intellect, and will. Therefore, we must reject all authoritative claims as so many acts of violence.

Of course, Christianity is inevitably caught up in the postmodern flight from authority. As the most powerful force shaping western culture, Christianity becomes the very essence of the authority against which we must protect ourselves. If we are afflicted with enduring divisions of race and class, then surely Christianity must have had a hand in causing this evil. If western societies subordinate women and deny them public roles, then again, Christianity must be the root of the problem. The list of particulars is endless, varying in focus according to the interests of critics, but the basic logic is always the same. The authority of the past must be overthrown; the sacred bonds of loyalty to what has been passed on must be broken, so that we can be released from the oppressive burdens of present power.

Anxieties about the closed circuit of dogma, the burdensome weight of tradition, and the crushing force of institutional authority lead our postmodern culture to the extreme of denying the authority

6. For a compelling account of the cultural sensibilities that form the defensive posture of postmodern humanism, see Philip Rieff, *The Triumph of the Therapeutic: Uses of Faith after Freud* (New York: Harper & Row, 1966). For Rieff, the therapeutic imperative has many facets, but it is unified in the overriding end sought: freedom from demand and interdiction, freedom from assent and commitment.

of truth itself. Our efforts to shield ourselves from coercive demand and its violence against individuality make us fear that some proposition, some insight, some conclusion to a syllogism, might gain control over our intellects and our souls. If any of us really believe that some proposition is true, then the diversity of our minds will fall victim to the uniformity of what is the case. Indeed, I am convinced that if the Vatican were to promulgate a document advising Catholic theologians that $2 + 2 = 4$, and that theologians are not to say otherwise if they wish to speak the truth, journalists would have no difficulty finding any number of sources who would denounce the authoritarian tone of such a directive.[7]

Such hyperbole can seem silly, but we should not underestimate the intensity of the postmodern horror of obedience, a horror that makes the power of truth itself a threat. "Sharing" now smothers debate. God forbid that anyone should formulate a reasoned argument; it might contradict or "marginalize" the experience of others. All sentences must begin with a compulsive ritual preface: "From my point of view. . . ." The truth and falsity of all claims depend upon one's "perspective." Everyone must be affirmed; the views of all must be validated.

Many of my colleagues in philosophy are convinced that this descent into the fog of all-views-are-equally-valid stems from a widespread belief in relativism. We are all, these professors imagine, in the grips of a bad theory of truth, and they spend a great deal of time trying to disabuse their students of this bad theory. The problem, however, is that this does not work. I can point out to my students that the truth that $2 + 2 = 4$ does not, in fact, depend upon anyone's point of view. I can expand upon the objectivity of the natural sciences. I can lecture about the distinction between truth and justification. I can exhort all to recognize that the possibilities of error and prejudice do not make them inevitable.

My efforts are in vain because my students have a primitive and unreflective commitment to the proposition that all truth is relative.

---

7. Recall, for example, the hue and cry surrounding the recent Vatican statement concerning interreligious and ecumenical dialogue, *Dominus Jesus*. The mere fact that the Congregation for the Doctrine of the Faith reiterated rather conventional Christian propositions about the uniqueness and necessity of Jesus Christ for salvation was sufficient to touch raw nerves. In the end, the offense is not *what* the Vatican teaches, but *that* she undertakes to state, with clarity, what is true and what is false.

They hold such a view as dogma, not as theory. It is a presupposition, not a conclusion. To be sure, sometimes they use the techniques of cultural critique. Truth claims, they say, are relative to their cultural contexts. If I press the issue and ask them to explain how such a view is consistent with the fact that modern science is practiced in India, Japan, Russia, and the United States, and that scientists go to international conferences and seem to agree with each other about all sorts of things regardless of cultural context, they look at me and shrug. At other times, they deploy sophistic tricks. A student insists that one cannot make non-mathematical claims about mathematics, and that this demonstrates that all systems of thought are closed and self-referential. Therefore, truth claims reduce to empty tautology. When I ask him in what sense the proposition that engineers find mathematics useful is a non-mathematical claim about mathematics, he just looks at me and repeats his conviction. His belief is more certain to him than anything I might say. It is a matter of faith, not evidence or inference.

These experiences in the classroom have convinced me that relativism is not a philosophical theory. It is a spiritual truth, a protective dogma designed to fend off any power that might claim our loyalty. It is a habit of mind that insulates postmodern life from the sober potency of arguments and the force of evidence, from the rightful claims of reason and the wisdom of the past. My students can look me in the eye and insist that one should never impose one's beliefs on others *and* that all truth claims, including, I presume, the moral rigorism of never, never imposing on others, are relative. Here, our contemporary horror of obedience joins hands with solipsism in order to protect the soul from all demands, rational or otherwise. Here, we are face to face with the spirit of our age.

A comparison of this outlook with the approach of modern humanism illustrates the striking shift from outward ambition to inward self-protection. For Kant, the traditional authority of Christian dogma must be rejected because it is indefensible. In its place we must put the proper and humanizing authority of the moral law, the truth of which is clear to practical reason, and the consequence of which is a restructuring of human society so as to respect and promote human dignity. In this way, the criticisms of Christian claims serve an aggressive project. Unjust and wrongful authority must give way to a just and proper authority that will usher in a new age. The false and debilitating authority of dogma must be renounced so that human beings can undertake the revolutions of genuine freedom based upon reason.

My students lack this rebellious spirit. Like so much of post-modern culture, their dispositions are submissive. They respect my authority as a teacher. They do not bridle against what they are told. They accept the fact that they must jump through educational hoops in order to get the professional certification they desire. They do not resent the harsh demands of the marketplace. They allow that governments must punish and imprison. In this sense, their critical spirit is not at all revolutionary. Their attitude is not Promethean. My students submit to the many demands of postmodern life, but with the knowing wink and sigh of a child raised on a steady diet of critique. They accept limitations, but they keep everything at a distance. This distance, and the many spiritual disciplines of postmodern life that deflect and demystify the powers that would penetrate into our lives, is the most fundamental form of postmodern humanism. It is a protective distance. In a society socialized to be non-judgmental, supported by the conviction that all truth is relative, the walls of defense against authority are strong indeed. We can safely navigate the danger of life, detached from the true and everlasting dangers of obedience and commitment, for nothing has the right to make a claim on our souls. Such is postmodern freedom.

III

Many cultural observers have noticed this spiritual detachment. Usually it is described as the postmodern stance of irony. There are now classical instances of such irony in the postmodern literature. Jacques Derrida's address to the *Société française de philosophie*, "Différance," is a particularly witty performance.[8] What Derrida says about what is written but cannot be heard launches a spiraling series of meditations that culminate in observations about the role of *différance* as the "ground of being." (I must use quotation marks, for in his essay, Derrida uses all metaphysical terms ironically.) I will not retrace the dialectical reductions, but will simply report Derrida's con-

---

8. The English translation may be found in *Margins of Philosophy*, trans. Alan Bass (Chicago: University of Chicago Press, 1982), pp. 1-27.

clusions. For Derrida, the power that produces meaning and claims of truth "governs nothing, and nowhere exercises authority. . . . Not only is there no kingdom of *différance*, but *différance* instigates the subversion of every kingdom" (p. 22). Roughly translated, Derrida is saying that our world is set in motion by power. Of that there is no doubt. But such power is originless and pointless. The order of things is a "bottomless chessboard on which Being is put into play" (p. 22). There is no beginning or end; there is no purpose or principle by which to regulate or judge the play.

"WHATEVER"

What is so important about Derrida is not the detail of his various literary performances. To imagine that deconstruction offers theoretical insight is to fall victim to just that which Derrida mocks.[9] Instead, the most telling aspect of Derrida's work is his spiritual advice. He does not rage against a meaningless cosmos. He does not adopt the young Sartre's existential determination in the face of a Godless world, and he certainly does not adopt the older Sartre's strategy of Marxist dogmatism. Instead, Derrida advises us to adopt light-heartedness. We should affirm the bottomless chessboard, he says, with "a certain laughter and a certain step of dance" (p. 27). In short, we should recognize that deconstruction, whatever that finally means in terms of theoretical commitments and interpretive performances, yields spiritual freedom. Nothing can sustain the burden of ultimate meaning or final truth, and therefore, nothing can rightfully put demands upon our soul.

In the hands of moralistic American critics, Derrida's work can take on ponderous significance. "Logocentrism" oppresses, and somehow, "difference" liberates. The old humanism mixes with the new, and messianic theorists imagine that the critical sophistication of postmodernism more effectively clears the ground for the proper demands of freedom and justice. However, Derrida's spiritual advice is far more widely followed than either the preaching of his moralistic disciples, or the theoretical twists and turns of his semiological method. To be sure, few break out into laughter and a dance. The stress and strain of postmodern life leaves little time for such indulgences. Nonetheless, the postmodern world cherishes the spiritual freedom

---

9. See Derrida's ironic comments about the "general strategy of deconstruction" and its status as a "science," in *Positions*, trans. Alan Bass (Chicago: University of Chicago Press, 1981), pp. 35-36, 41-42.

that Derrida rightly identifies as the fruit of deconstruction. Ironic detachment, the smirk of critical tropes, the serene complacency made possible by the dogmatic belief that all truth is relative: these and other habits of mind keep our souls free from the disturbing need to change.

We should forswear conspiracy theories. Whatever we might imagine that Derrida represents — cynical French intellectual life, decadent academic self-indulgence, ruthless Nietzschean will-to-power — none of these things have caused or even influenced the world in which I live and work. My students certainly lack any knowledge of Derrida, and they could not begin to recapitulate the analysis of postmodern literary theory. Yet, they are surprisingly close to his conclusions. Their relativism is painfully unsophisticated, but it serves the same purpose as Derrida's elaborate theoretical machinery. Their dogmatic conviction that truth is not really possible serves to promote spiritual freedom. Of course, we must live according to countless rules; yet, guided by the therapy of critique and buttressed by a dogmatic relativism, the chessboard is bottomless. In such a world, delicious irony keeps us afloat.

IV

If I am correct in reading the signs of the times, then the spirit of our postmodern age is Petronian, not Promethean, and this makes a great difference when we undertake to preach the gospel. Petronius was an enigmatic Roman who lived during the time of Nero. His notorious observations of Roman aristocratic life come down to us in the *Satyricon*, a rambling narrative that is part soap opera, part *National Enquirer* article, and part modern social criticism. In the *Satyricon*, Petronius is a participant who stands at one remove. He is an observer who can mock and satirize. He can describe venality without judgment; he can narrate vice without protest. In these ways, Petronius exemplifies the spiritual ideal that now dominates postmodern western culture. He creates a pervasive atmosphere of superficiality that drains all spiritual significance from events. His characters are realistic, yet they are spectral, soulless creatures who utterly lack gravity. Never moralistic, never interjecting with the voice of some loftier vision, Petronius simply drains all power from social life. It is not sufficiently real, not sufficiently thick and weighty, to disrupt the equilib rium of the soul. For this reason, as both writer and participant, Petronius is in the world but not of the world. Yet his freedom has nothing to do with the ascetical disciplines that detach the Christian from the world. Instead, Petronius enjoys a spiritual freedom similar to the dance and laugh advocated by Derrida. It is the freedom that comes from the confidence that there is no Lord of life, from the wry certainty that the world is carried forward on the currents of instinct, venality, and conceit.

Postmodern culture achieves the same effect with its many and diverse moral disciplines. We must "share" rather than debate. We are trained to be non-judgmental. The dogma of relativism surrounds us with reassuring doubt. The postmodern culture of critique turns everything into a shadow and shade. Genealogical reduction drains the blood out of present forms of life. Everything around us is weightless, leaving us free to be ourselves. And even our inner lives of anxiety and self-doubt are carefully stilled as we seek a therapeutic equilibrium. The upshot is a Petronian humanism. We cultivate a cynicism that does not despair, because it serves to destroy the charms of truth and beauty that might corrupt our inner peace. We enjoy an irony that does not seek resolution, because it supports our desire to be invulnerable observers rather than participants at risk. We are spectators of our own lives, free from the strain of drama and the uncertainty of a story in which our souls are at stake. We conform because nothing finally matters except the superiority of knowing it to be so.

As I suggested earlier, modern humanism and its ambitions on behalf of freedom and reason often tempted theologians into various alliances. Ill-advised or not, these alliances depended upon a shared ambition, a shared joy in the promise of changes that would shape the soul. Emerson wished to clear away false dependency upon external authority so that the voice of conscience could govern and transform. Locke hoped to set us on the sure path of clear thinking. Any Christian preacher worth his salt, whether borrowing from this humanist tradition or not, preaches repentance, wishing to turn those who listen away from sin and toward righteousness. Change is at the heart of the gospel. At this strange juncture in human history, we need to realize that old debates about which way to turn for the power that might effect change — toward inner human potencies or toward the power of God in Christ — are now moot. Instead, the present age wishes to insulate itself against any call to turn, either for or against: postmodern culture keeps all demands for change at a distance. Postmodern humanism does not want to shoulder the gospel out of the center of life so the human potencies might burst forth from the chrysalis of ancient dogma or traditional morality. Quite the contrary, this Petronian humanism wishes to neuter all power and potency, human or otherwise. No dynamism is allowed to penetrate the defenses of irony, satire, and critical sophistication. The soul must remain unaltered, unaffected.

V

The western theological tradition is keyed to the challenges of Promethean ambition, not Petronian apathy. We are the inheritors of that tradition, and as a consequence, we can mistakenly respond to the postmodern age. Cynicism can seem like a gain for the gospel. After all, the New Testament counsels Christians to take a jaundiced view of worldly wisdom. Furthermore, irony can appear to be an ally, for the postmodern reluctance to adopt the old humanistic projects with wholehearted vigor, whether Emersonian or Lockean, suggests a newfound humility. Finally, the willing conformity that characterizes so much of postmodern life can give the evangelist hope that the prideful self-sufficiency of modernity has finally exhausted itself. These are, however, deceptions made possible by a fixation on pride as the primary barrier to faith. Sloth and cowardice, however, are just as deadly. Both slink away from the urgency of conviction. Both fear the sharp edge of demand and expectation. Both have a vested interest in cynicism, irony, and outward conformity. These vices, not pride, now dominate our culture.

What do the vices of sloth and cowardice mean for evangelism in the postmodern context? How does this Petronian humanism and its commitment to spiritual freedom shape the challenges of preaching and teaching the gospel in our age? I am a university professor who observes his students and tries to orient himself in the increasingly strange landscape of this third millennium. I am not engaged in pastoral work, at least not in the primary sense of ordering the community of the faithful in worship. Nonetheless, in my own pedagogy, I am constantly trying to penetrate the defenses of irony; I am always attempting to bridge the seemingly depthless chasms of critique. Furthermore, I am more a child of this age than I would like to admit. Petronius is closer kin than Prometheus, and to the extent that I know my own resistances to the gospel, I have some small insights into the pastoral challenges. Therefore, I will venture a brief observation.

No moderation of the demands of the gospel will satisfy the postmodern spirit. To a great extent, the modern project of apologetics involved trying to accentuate the humanistic dimension of the gospel. As I have suggested already, the redemptive promise of Christianity parallels the modern concern about freedom. Moreover, the strong claims of dogma are not dissimilar to the ways in which modern science insists upon obedience to evidence and argument. For this reason, evangelism could undertake to redirect the passions of modernity toward the proper end of faith in Christ. The deepest hopes of modernity may find their fulfillment in the gospel. Yet, if I am correct in my analysis, postmodern culture no longer nurtures hope in the human heart. Quite the contrary, it promises quiescent freedom from the disturbances of expectations and demands. For this reason, the gospel of redemption will be an offense, no matter how carefully modulated, no matter how cleverly dressed up in the finery of modern ideals of freedom and rational responsibility. Therefore, evangelism has no reason to hide the hard demands of the gospel.

John Paul II is a signal example in our own time. *Veritatis Splendor,* the encyclical concerning moral theology, warns against the dangers of moral relativism and subjectivism. What is striking about *Veritatis Splendor,* however, is not its polemic against moral relativism. After all, as I have said, my philosophy colleagues do as much in their classes. Instead, the extraordinary aspect is the view of freedom it advances, a view utterly at odds with the spiritual freedom so cherished by our age. The encyclical ends with a meditation on the Virgin Mary. She is commended as the exemplar of Christian freedom, and that freedom has the following form. Called to serve the LORD with body and soul, she gave herself in obedience to a demand the scope and import of which she did not understand.

The upshot is more than the leverage that moral right and wrong gives us against our bondage to worldly powers. For John Paul II, the Virgin Mary is the model of Christian moral obedience because she has the courage of obedience to those disciplines and sacrifices that do not yield just a freedom from sin, but a freedom for supernatural life. Only by taking the severe and dangerous risks of obedience to something beyond our comprehension can we have the freedom to participate in divine glory. For this reason, Christian freedom requires a spiritual ambition that is very much at odds with the postmodern age. Such ambition does not throw up protective walls to block the demands of the gospel. Instead, spiritual ambition forsakes prerogatives, renounces the rights and privileges of intellect and will. All defenses to the transforming power of grace are removed, even those that emerge out of the rightful worries we all have about dominion and deception. Only in this way, says John Paul II, echoing St. Augustine, can we draw near to the power of life. After all, Christian ambition is supernatural precisely because it seeks to become more than that which human power can produce.

The moral challenge of evangelism is, then, to nurture an ambition that has the courage of obedience, the courage to draw as near as possible to redemptive power by tearing down the walls of defense. Without doubt, this can be done in any number of ways, but I wish to end this essay with a final word. It is a hard truth that pastors know but do not wish to hear: unless you preach chastity, and not the easy chastity of sex governed by commitment and love, but the hard chastity taught by St. Paul, you will fail to meet the moral challenge of evangelism in this postmodern age. This is not because sex is the most important dimension of the Christian life; it is because sexual freedom is the most cherished and most Petronian moral commitment of the postmodern age. Our age runs from chastity for the same reason that St. Augustine, in his *Confessions,* reports that he always ended his prayer for chastity with the plea, "But not yet!"[10] As St. Augustine knew, if we can change this altogether fundamental part of our lives, a part woven into the fabric of instinct, then the defenses against redemptive change are down. If the perfectly normal and natural needs of the body can be directed toward God, then surely the higher faculties of will and intellect can as well.

On this point, as on so many, St. Augustine is surely right. It is not an accident that those who have the least immediate and instinctual interest in resisting the classical Christian teaching on sexual morality — aged clerics — often offer the most ardent defenses of the rights and prerogatives of the libido. Bishop Spong loves his freedom as much as my twenty-year-old students, indeed, more so because the

10. Book VIII, Chapter 7.

love has become both more habitual and more spiritual. God forbid that my needs might be stymied, my impulses denied! God forbid that I should have to bring my reason to the authority of God's Word. God forbid that I should have to submit the raw material of my life to God so that I might be melted down and reformed into something very different. God forbid that I should have to change. We defend ourselves against chastity, not because we are prideful and self-confident hedonists, not because we take great joy from the confusing labyrinths of sexual desire and satisfaction, but because we are fearful that, once the invasion of grace begins, it will not relent until the capitol falls. We embrace sexual freedom because it is a crucial line of defense against transformative demands.

My students may not know Derrida, but they are not fools. They well know that the imperative of Christian chastity is a direct assault on what is forbidden by the Petronian humanism of our postmodern age: allowing ideals to enter into our souls in order to reshape our identities. It is a direct assault upon our spiritual freedom, but not because it involves restraint and limitation. I must reiterate. My students know and accept the many restraints that society imposes upon them. Chastity is an assault from which they recoil in horror because, to the twenty-year-old mind, it is so insanely ambitious, so hopelessly impossible, so ruthlessly physical *and* personal. At this point, my students may understand next to nothing about the Christian ascetical tradition, its goals and methods, as well as the relation between self-denial and God's intentions for our salvation. These are matters I am not sure that I understand. But of this I *am* sure. In their recoil from chastity, they have difficulty maintaining Petronian equilibrium. It is difficult to contemplate chastity with "a laugh and a step of dance." It is a moment when their Petronian humanism shouts "No" without a wink or a nod of irony. In chastity, they hear a word that is a sharp and two-edged sword.

The Powerlessness of Talking Heads: Re-Evangelization in a Postmodern World — The Place of Ethics

PHILIP TURNER

> See, just as the Lord my God has charged me, I now teach you statutes and ordinances for you to observe in the land that you are about to enter and occupy. You must observe them diligently, for this will show your wisdom and discernment to the peoples, who, when they hear all these statutes, will say, "Surely this great nation is a wise and discerning people!" For what other great nation has a god so near to it as the Lord our God is whenever we call to him? And what other great nation has statutes and ordinances as just as this entire law that I am setting before you today?
>
> Deuteronomy 4:5-8

Introduction

To give some idea of the direction in which this essay is heading, allow me to begin with a comment on the title of this book: "The Strange New Word of the Gospel: Re-Evangelizing in the Postmodern World." Generalizations are very dangerous things, but I suspect that the reactions of a large number of "mainline" Protestants to each of the title's key words will be rather different. The word "postmodern" will, on the whole, have a positive ring. It will call to mind apologetic strategies that bring the churches into dialogue with a challenging and often exciting cultural trend — one that liberates us from the "logocentric" dogmas of the past, creates a culture of diversity, and sets us off on a journey of self-discovery. The word "re-evangelizing," on the other hand, will prove less inviting. At best, it will connote church growth. At a deeper and even less inviting level, it will call to mind the saccharine world of televangelists and, at a deeper level still, that great American religious tragedy — the long, agonizing, and often shameful debate between fundamentalists and modernists.

Reactions to "postmodern" and "re-evangelizing" will be immediate and, with a moment's thought, recognizable. Responses to "the strange new word" will be slower, more subterranean, and more disturbing. Why "the *strange* new word"? After all, the evangelistic strategy that comes most easily to the minds of the inhabitants of the "mainline" churches is one of the apologetic recognition of our truth within the best insights of the movements of culture that define the spirit of our age. To speak of a "strange new word" appears to call into question our basic stance in relation to the culture that envelops and shapes us, and for this reason such speech is, at a minimum, disturbing.

I have not been privy to the thoughts and intentions of those who planned this conference, but I have assumed that, in assigning this title to their efforts they intended to create just such a disturbance. I have assumed that they intended to call for an unfamiliar, indeed unattractive, effort (re-evangelization) that presupposes not a bridge but a gulf between a "word" spoken and the pattern of speech and life we associate with "the postmodern world." If such was their intention, I wish at the outset to signal my agreement and, if it was not, I can only say that I wish it had been. For I believe that re-evangelization in the postmodern world involves the presentation of a counter-reality — one that, not in all ways but in certain particular ways, indeed comes as a "strange new word." In short, I believe that re-evangelization, should the effort be undertaken, involves something more akin to a confrontation between contending forces than it does a conversation between people who basically agree but must clear up a few misunderstandings and confusions.

In making a statement like this, I am well aware that I place myself at cross-purposes with the tradition of apologetic theology that so characterizes the more contemporary views of evangelization held by members of my own, Episcopal, church. Given that fact, let it be said that I do not wish to dispute the value of apologetic theology as such. I just don't believe it constitutes the basic means of evangelism. In fact, I have come to believe that apologetic theology works better with believers who are having intellectual problems with their faith or their church than it does with nonbelievers.[1] It may be that a more aggressive stance is needed to get the attention of the latter.

I hasten to add that taking an aggressive stance does not require the substitution of a message of "fire and brimstone" for the gospel of mercy. It does, however, require a different perception of what goes on in the process of communicating the gospel message. It may require a less irenic view of what transpires when the gospel is proclaimed, be it in the modern world, the pre-modern world, or the postmodern world. No less a figure than Hendrik Kraemer reminded us some forty-five years ago of this fact about the communication of the gospel:

> But being the message of the cross, of the mysterious wisdom of God, which acts as the saving power of God, precisely for this reason it is a scandal to all self-confident human wisdom. It is not according to, but against, human nature, although it is the only power capable of converting man into his true, God-willed nature.[2]

In a way that, if understood, would be simply devastating to most forms of American Christianity, he went on to insist that, "The search for successful communication has no Biblical justification. Only the search for faithful, really interpretative communication has."[3] Offensive as it may be to our ears, Kraemer argued that in considering the

---

1. I do not mean to say either that something like John Howard Yoder's "*ad hoc* apologetics" might not prove useful in arguing with believers and nonbelievers alike. There are indeed values "out there" that believers and nonbelievers alike share and on occasion appeal can and should be made to them. I mean only that even an *ad hoc* apologetic will not prove itself the basic medium for a communication of the gospel message that ends in conversion and entry into the common life of the church. For Yoder's discussion of apologetics see John Howard Yoder, *The Priestly Kingdom: Social Ethics as Gospel* (Notre Dame, Ind.: University of Notre Dame Press, 1984), pp. 40-43.

2. Hendrik Kraemer, *The Communication of the Christian Faith* (Philadelphia: Westminster, 1956), p. 29.

3. Kraemer, *The Communication of the Christian Faith*, p. 30.

communication of the Christian gospel, one could not be sanguine. It is essential, he said, to take account of what the Bible calls "hardened hearts." And then he said this:

> This persistent occurrence in the Bible of cardiosclerosis as a negative response to God or as an act of divine judgment points to the "mystery of iniquity" in the world, the realm of demonic power to which man can deliver himself and thus make himself inaccessible to communication of the Christian message. . . . We have to make the observation that it is in relation to the communication of the Christian message only that the mysterious thing happens: communication as a means of its annihilation. If there is a proof for the contention . . . that communication is not only a psychological matter but ultimately a metaphysical or theological matter, it is precisely this fact of cardiosclerosis.[4]

That is one way to put it. Another is to say that the cross is central to the evangel, and as such the evangel brings to light enmity between God and us that cannot be reconciled by the blandishments of cogent argument. Accordingly, to speak either of evangelization or re-evangelization is to speak of conflict in which the truth about God in Christ runs up against and sets in bold relief truth as we would have it. For this reason alone, re-evangelization requires more than what I have called "talking heads." By this term of art I mean that re-evangelization requires more than carefully measured argument uttered by people who inhabit what might be called "a virtual world," by people who in no way have to live the life of which they speak. Re-evangelization requires more than words. It requires as well an alternative way of life. This way of life at one and the same time gives concrete expression to the word spoken and by its very contrariness exposes our endemic resistance to God's rightful claim upon our lives. In a way that I hope to make plain, re-evangelization requires us to reunite those two long lost siblings — theology and ethics — in a common witness to something quite contrary to postmodernism, namely, truth.

---

4. Kraemer, *The Communication of the Christian Faith*, p. 31.

The Gospel, Evangelization, the Postmodern World: What on Earth Do We Mean?

Before I come to the heart of my argument, a word, though only a brief one, must be spoken about the subject matter before us, namely, "the gospel," "re-evangelization," and "the postmodern world." In our time, there is not a single one of these terms whose meaning is uncontested. As a result, we could spend all our time arguing over what we are talking about. I propose instead to say only enough to make clear what I take their meaning to be.

As for "the gospel," the ways in which we use and understand the term have been horribly deformed by the long battle between liberals and evangelicals. In his opening address at the 1966 congress on evangelism held in Berlin, Billy Graham noted that the secretary of one of America's most established denominations had made the following statement:

> The redemption of the world is not dependent upon the souls we win for Christ. . . . There cannot be individual salvation. . . . Salvation has more to do with the whole society than with the individual soul. . . . We must not be satisfied to win people one by one. . . . Contemporary evangelism is moving away from winning souls one by one to the evangelization of the structures of society.[5]

This church official's comment pertained to evangelism, but behind it stands a view that defines the gospel as good news about God's purpose to create a more just social order. In reaction, evangelicals, in their discussions of the mission of the churches, felt required to give increased emphasis to what now is called "social ministry." Nevertheless, they continued to insist that the gospel is not in the first instance a message about the reformation of social order. Rather, it is one about the salvation of souls.[6] In Graham's words, the message of evangelism is contained in Paul's summary, "For I delivered unto you first of all that which I also received, how that Christ died for our sins according to the scriptures; and that he was buried, and that he rose

---

5. Billy Graham, "Why the Berlin Congress?" in *One Race, One Gospel, One Task (Vol. 1): World Congress of Evangelism. Berlin 1966 Official Reference Volumes: Papers and Reports* (Minneapolis: World Wide Publications, 1967), p. 24.

6. See, e.g., *The New Face of Evangelicalism: An International Symposium on the Lausanne Covenant*, ed. C. René Padilla (Downers Grove, Ill.: InterVarsity, 1976).

again on the third day according to the scriptures."[7] This is the
evangel, and it is to be preached with a view toward the conversion
and salvation of sinners.

To the liberal mind, the gospel message as presented by evangelicals gives too little attention to God's redemption of the social order.
To those of a more evangelical persuasion, the gospel as presented by
liberals gives too little attention to the cross as a divine act of judgment and mercy that sets people free from the powers of sin and death
that separate them from God. Having read back over the literature of
this debate, I came away convinced that, with some notable excep-
tions, neither side wishes to discount completely the concerns of the
other. Indeed, one finds people normally thought to be poles apart
saying things that are surprisingly similar. Thus, Gustavo Gutiérrez,
the *doyen* of liberation theology, insists that liberation from sin is the
first and basic step in the process of social liberation. In his *A Theology
of Liberation* Gutiérrez writes as follows:

> In the Bible, Christ is presented as the one who brings us liberation.
> Christ the Savior liberates man from sin which is the ultimate root of
> all disruption of friendship and all injustice and oppression. Christ
> makes man truly free, that is to say, he enables man to live in commu-
> nion with him; and this is the basis for all human brotherhood.[8]

Compare the statement by Gutiérrez with one made by no less an
evangelical than Carl Henry at the Berlin Congress in 1966.

> The Christian evangelist has a message doubly relevant to the mod-
> ern scene: he knows that *justice* is due all because a just God created
> mankind in his holy image, and he knows that all men need *justifica-
> tion* because the Holy Creator sees us as rebellious sinners. The Gos-
> pel is good news not simply because it reinforces modern man's lost
> sense of personal worth and confirms the demand for universal jus-
> tice on the basis of creation, but also because it offers rebellious men
> as doomed sinners that justification and redemption without which
> no man can see God and live.[9]

7. Billy Graham, "Why the Berlin Congress?" pp. 28-29.
8. Gustavo Gutiérrez, *A Theology of Liberation: History, Politics and Salvation* (Maryknoll, N.Y.: Orbis Books, 1973), p. 37.
9. Carl Henry, "Facing a New Day in Evangelism," in *One Race, One Gospel, One Task*,
p. 16.

Gutiérrez and Henry make strange bedfellows. Remarkably, these statements show that they are not as far apart as one might at first imagine. Neither wishes to jettison the chief concern of the other. They do, however, have serious differences, not only about the proper theological locus of a concern for justice but also about the heart of the gospel itself.[10] Is the gospel in the first instance good news about God's plans for the social order or is it in the first instance good news about his purposes for the souls of sinners? Gutiérrez places emphasis on the first and Henry on the second. My own view is that, though neither wishes to discount the case of the other, in the end both sell short the content of the gospel message. It is much more richly layered and thickly textured than either allows.

The gospel is a complex message in the form of a narrative account of who God is and what God is up to that includes but far exceeds either the liberal or the evangelical gospel. I take it that the good news is summed up in the great creeds of the church which confess that the biblical narrative renders for us *one* God whom we know as Father, Son, and Holy Spirit, who (alone) created the worlds, who elected Israel as his special people so that all peoples would come to know and love the one true God, who in the fullness of time sent his Son to reconcile through his sacrificial death the peoples of the earth and to restore the order of creation. This Son ascended to the right hand of God, the Father, who sent the Spirit to those who receive the Son and bound them together in his body the church, who will come again to judge the peoples of the earth and who, through the Spirit, will bring all things to their intended end and perfection.

The previous sentence is "run on" to an extraordinary degree, but it takes a "run-on sentence" to capture the full extent of the good news of God in Christ, and it is just this "run-on sentence" that, in our time, exposes the truncated and inadequate version of the good news that characterizes both liberals and evangelicals. I know also that I need to say why I believe that the good news is comprised of this entire narrative rather than one part of it, but that enterprise will have to wait for another occasion. For the moment, I wish to note only the obvious fact that the contrasting views of the gospel held by liberals and

10. Henry is quite insistent that a concern for justice should be located within the doctrine of creation. Gutiérrez, on the other hand, locates a concern for justice first within the doctrine of redemption. It is this theological difference that lies behind the different emphases and treatments they give the question of justice.

evangelicals give rise to two views of evangelization. One focuses on raising consciousness so that people see God's purposes for the social order and join in efforts to achieve these goals. The other focuses on proclaiming a message of personal salvation that will lead people to a living faith in Christ and a new form of life.

Professor William Abraham has, however, suggested a more inclusive definition — one I believe to be in keeping with the more expansive definition of the gospel previously suggested. He understands evangelism as "primary initiation into the kingdom of God."[11] It is an activity that depends upon three assumptions that together provide a shorthand version of the entire gospel narrative as I have presented it. The assumptions are (1) God is a transcendent agent, (2) God acts in the life of his people Israel and in the coming of the kingdom in the life of Jesus, and (3) the claims of the kingdom involve a future dimension.[12] Further, evangelism is an activity that contains within it a complex of activities, viz., proclamation, inclusion into the community of the church, owning certain intellectual claims, appropriation of a moral vision, recognition and reception of certain gifts and capacities (of the Spirit), and acceptance of forms of communal and individual discipline.[13]

Professor Abraham is a Protestant and it is perhaps for this reason that he employs the term "evangelism" rather than the term preferred by those of a more "catholic" persuasion — "evangelization." Protestant roots provide the only reason I can think of for his preference for the term "evangelism" since, in using the term, he speaks of it in precisely the way in which more "catholic" voices speak of "evangelization." The terminology is not the important matter, however. Indeed, I have never been certain why one term is used rather than the other because, in the end, everyone ends up talking about the same complex that Professor Abraham tracks. I suspect, however, that those who speak of "evangelism" wish to place emphasis on proclamation that leads to a particular event — conversion. Those who speak of "evangelization" wish to emphasize the fact that becoming a Christian is a process whose various aspects are separated only at

11. William Abraham, *The Logic of Evangelism* (London: Hodder & Stoughton, 1989), p. 13.
12. Abraham, *The Logic of Evangelism*, p. 20.
13. For Abraham's discussion of these matters see *The Logic of Evangelism*, pp. 101-3.

great peril. They may as well wish to include in their notion the "Christianizing" of a culture.

The organizers of this conference have chosen to use the term evangelization and, with one exception to normal usage, I happily join them in this usage. For practical reasons, I do not believe that "re-evangelization" in the postmodern world of America will lead to "re-Christianizing" American culture. I shall say more about my reasons for this conclusion later in this paper. At this point, however, I would like to make it clear that I harbor no animus against the project of Christianizing a culture. Indeed, I agree with Prof. O'Donovan: at an earlier period of the church's history, the creation of a Christian society constituted a godly response to God's action in Christ.[14] As I have said, however, I do not believe this particular aspect of evangelization ought to be a primary focus of energy for the churches in America at this particular juncture of history. To focus attention on "a cultural mission" will deflect from what I take to be the real task at hand, namely, to constitute the churches in such a way that people can be formed as Christians in the midst of a social order that is not friendly to such an enterprise. Such formation, it seems to me, is a necessary precondition for undertaking anything like a "cultural mission."[15]

With this proviso in mind, I think it best to speak of re-evangelization rather than re-evangelism. I do so because I believe that re-evangelization like evangelization requires one to view conversion not as a single event but as a complex process that moves through the steps Professor Abraham has outlined. So I hold that both the evangel and re-evangelization are more complex notions and more complex activities than popular usage now allows.

But what about "the postmodern world" in which re-evangelization is to take place. How shall we understand this venue? The first thing to say, of course, is that the very character of postmodernism makes an activity like "re-evangelization" extraordi-

---

14. See, i.e., Oliver O'Donovan, *The Desire of the Nations: Rediscovering the Roots of Political Theology* (Cambridge: Cambridge University Press, 1996).

15. I should also like to make it clear that I do not believe a "cultural mission" falls to the church as one of the many institutions within a social order. If there is something like a "cultural mission," it falls to Christians as Christians living out their vocations within the social order in which they find themselves. A self-understanding of this sort on the part of an ecclesial institution always proves pretentious and always ends in an unhealthy clericalism.

narily suspect, and one is forced to admit that the "mainline" churches share the suspicions of their environing culture. Why this suspicion? Use of the term re-evangelization, oddly enough, leads to an answer in that it suggests an original evangelization that has "gone south" and left behind only traces of what used to be. "Re-evangelization" suggests, therefore, the restoration of a unity of faith and practice and so a unity of culture that now exists only in traces and memories. "Re-evangelization" thus serves by contrast to display the defining feature of postmodernism, namely, a "de-centering" that refuses to give pride of place to any one set of beliefs or any single way of life. As Richard Rorty has so ably argued, the privileged form of speech in a postmodern world should be "dialogue" rather than proclamation. The chief virtue should be tolerance rather than zeal for the truth.[16] The devotees of any system of beliefs should forswear evangelism (or evangelization) in the name of peaceful coexistence within a pluralistic social order and within a pluralistic ideational world whose diversity is intractable.

If he means what he says, it would appear that the presiding bishop of my own, Episcopal, church, who speaks repeatedly about a plurality of truths, has adopted Rorty's position, and I assume that among both the leaders and the rank and file of our various churches he is not alone. So we should be clear from the outset that to speak of "re-evangelizing in the postmodern world" is to run across not only the emergent mind of the church in our time and place but also the fundamental premise of the postmodern world. To speak of or engage in re-evangelization is to engage in a very "un-postmodern activity" that may well call down the ire of both society and the established leadership of the "mainline" churches.

The Powerlessness of Talking Heads

Contrary to the basic assumption of the postmodern world, I believe that Christians must assume that the gospel narrative is true, that our lives in a most fundamental way depend upon holding to that truth in

16. Professor Rorty has argued his views in many places and in many ways, but to my mind the best presentation remains *Contingency, Irony and Solidarity* (Cambridge: Cambridge University Press, 1989).

obedient faith, that the truth made known in Christ Jesus is a matter of life and death, that it is a truth worth dying for, and that as a consequence we are constrained both by love of God and love of neighbor to bear witness to what we hold to be true.[17] The question is then how that witness is to take place in a postmodern world — in a world where any truth claim is by nature suspect.

As an introduction to my response to the question, allow me to share a story. During the 1960s I was a missionary of the Episcopal Church serving in Uganda. Toward the end of that time, it was my privilege to chair a conference, the purpose of which was to bring about a temporary ceasefire in the war that had raged there since the early 1960s. At one of the breaks in these discussions, I was able to speak with a pastor who served as chaplain to one of the largest Southern armies. I asked him how things fared for the church and he responded that things went well. "They always go well when we suffer," he said. "The bad times come when things become easy for us." I then asked him how many people he had baptized over the past year. He thought for a moment and then answered, "About 10,000!" After taking time to recover, I managed to ask if he had any idea why so many conversions had occurred. I expected him to speak about how hard the times were and how people needed a redeemer in such times. Instead, he said that many of the conversions occurred because people noticed a palpable difference in the way Christian men treated their wives and they were attracted to a religion that made such an obvious and important difference.

In telling this story, I in no way mean to suggest that the basic

plausibility

17. As the argument of this paper unfolds, it will become clear that I hold to a view of the nature of Christian truth that is close to that presented in George Lindbeck's *The Nature of Doctrine*. By his own admission, Lindbeck's "cultural/linguistic" account of the nature of doctrine, with its emphasis on "intra-textuality," is itself thoroughly postmodern. Lindbeck's form of postmodernism, however, is realist in its view of truth. His realism suggests that there are forms of "postmodernism" which Christians may embrace without surrendering all truth claims. There are indeed things helpful to the theological enterprise to be learned from some forms of postmodernism. Thus, when speaking in this paper of "a postmodern world" I use the phrase as a term of art to indicate a popular view of human language and culture that seeks to exile truth claims from the public arena and contain them within the realm of private belief and opinion. For a helpful discussion of the possible ways in which a "postmodern" view of the nature of doctrine can be linked with a realist view of truth see Sue Patterson, *Realist Christian Theology in a Postmodern Age* (Cambridge: Cambridge University Press, 1999).

message of the preaching common at that time and in that place was of little importance. Indeed, the standard sermon in East Africa in those days centered on Christ's sacrificial death — a death that procured the forgiveness of sins and allowed for reconciliation between warring parties. In various ways, this aspect of the good news found a "point of contact" within the societies of East and Central Africa. What I find interesting, however, is that a new form of relationship between husbands and wives, one that reflected the forgiveness and reconciliation thought to lie at the heart of the gospel, was the factor cited to explain a startling number of conversions. What I have termed "talking heads," in the eyes of the pastor of whom I spoke, lacked power apart from the clear example of lives lived.

This pastor's observation of contemporary conversions bears a marked resemblance to an observation George Lindbeck has made about conversions in the early church.

> Pagan converts to the catholic mainstream did not, for the most part, first understand the faith and then decide to become Christians; rather, the process was reversed: they first decided and then they understood. More precisely, they were first attracted by the Christian community and form of life.[18]

Now, at last, I have reached the central point of this essay. Christian ethics are not consequent either to evangelization or re-evangelization any more than (*pace* C. H. Dodd) *didache* is consequent to *kerygma* — they are in certain ways central to the entire complex of activities that comprise the process that Professor Abraham has so ably displayed. To place such emphasis on "works" is bound to cause more than a little discomfort, particularly among Protestants of a Lutheran persuasion. My hope, however, is that a brief bible study will make plain the precise nature of this claim and perhaps even serve to allay anxiety. To argue my point I could turn easily to the Gospels of Matthew or John, or the Book of Acts or Romans or Corinthians. I have chosen instead to provide a reading of the Epistle to the Ephesians, and I have done so simply because this letter will allow me to accomplish my task more briefly and more efficiently.

---

18. George Lindbeck, *The Nature of Doctrine* (Philadelphia: Westminster Press, 1984), p. 132.

"Paul's" View of the Place of Ethics in the Life of the Church

Most I think would agree that the central point of this letter is the great purpose of God to unite the peoples of the earth through the reconciling sacrifice of Christ (Eph. 1:9-10; 2:13-22). This purpose has been God's from the beginning, but it has now been made known through Christ to the church. Further, it is through the ministry of the Apostle Paul and the life of the churches that resulted from his preaching that the purposes of God are to become visible within the creation with such clarity and force that the peoples of the earth will see what God's plan for creation is. Indeed, even the heavenly powers, the powers that, prior to the coming of Christ, ruled over the peoples of the earth, are to see through the visible unity of the church that they no longer have power to rule, divide, and destroy (Eph. 3:9-11).

The Letter to the Ephesians contains no command to go into all the world and preach the gospel. Indeed, its subject matter dwells heavily on the interior life of the church. Nevertheless, what we are calling "evangelization" seems to underwrite most of what it has to say about both God and the church. It is both the purpose of God to reunite the peoples and it is the calling of the church to manifest that unity for all to see. It is not surprising, therefore, that the nature of the church is described in relation to its calling. The church is said to be a new humankind or *Adam,* a single body that has many members but one head (Christ), fellow citizens of a single commonwealth, members of a single household of which God is the father, and the temple of the Lord, the place where, through the Spirit, God is present at the very center of the earth (Eph. 2:15-22; 4:11-16).

Given this high calling and given this exemplary nature, it is not surprising that the author's final exhortation begins by urging the saints to whom he writes to live a life "worthy" *(axios)* of the unity to which they have been called (Eph. 4:1).[19] The gospel message of rec-

---

19. The Greek word *axios* to be sure means "worthy," but it is also the case that it carries the connotation of "proportionate." Thus, in calling for a worthy life the author calls for a life that in its way is proportionate not only to the calling of the church but also to the life of Christ which is to be "imitated" by believers in their relations one with another and with those who do not believe. The notion of worthiness, therefore, suggests a form of imitation that is not identical with its archetype but like it in relevant respects.

onciliation through the cross is to be reflected in the common life of the church that is to be both the place where God's purpose for the creation is being realized and a palpable witness to this purpose and its realization. Thus, in spelling out the sort of life that is worthy of God's calling, the author of Ephesians links the secret *(mystērion)* of God's purpose made known in Christ with the life of the church which is to exemplify it. Accordingly, in spelling out the sort of life that is worthy of God's calling, the author of this letter not only urges a particular form of behavior, he also gives specific content to the sort of unity God has in mind. It is a unity of persons, each of whom has a particular gift to offer within the communion of saints (Eph. 4:11-16). It is also a unity that can be characterized by the presence of certain powers of soul within the "body" or "household" or "temple" and certain common practices which, in combination, give love — the basis of unity — a recognizable face. These powers of soul and practices all imitate the sacrificial life of Christ and can be adumbrated as follows: a certain humility of mind *(tapeinophrosunē)*, a sort of respectfulness toward others that treats them as if they were one's betters *(prautēs)*, and a degree of patience *(makrothumia)* that manifests itself in putting up with difficult people *(anechomai)* out of love *(agapē)* for them (Eph. 4:1-2). Such love, which provides both the basis and the content of the unity God seeks, also manifests itself in being kind *(chrēstos)* and compassionate *(eusplanchnos)* and in being mutually forgiving of wrongs done *(charizomai)* (Eph. 4:32).

These practices and powers of soul give content to what it is to walk in love and to walk in a way worthy of the calling of the church. They also give credibility to the announcement of the great mystery that has been revealed. They make visible in a believable manner the way in which Christ loved us and gave himself for us as an offering and sacrifice to God (Eph. 4:1; 5:1). They manifest the new nature of the new humankind (Eph. 4:24) and so also become the way Adam once more imitates or becomes the image of God (Eph. 1:19).

After rehearsing this account of Christian ethics and their place within God's providential purposes, it is easy to see why Ephesians is noted for its "realized eschatology." Once noted, this rather high-flying account of the Christian life and the life of the church is often cited as a reason for dismissing this letter, but what commentators seem always to miss is that these eschatological powers are said to be present in the midst of an ongoing conflict that cuts through the spirit of each person, the life of the church, and the life of the "world" it is God's purpose to reconcile. One can interpret the admonitions found in the letter to "put off" one form of life and "put on" another only as indications that what might be called an old form of life lingers on even in the church. These admonitions indicate also that God's purposes become manifest within history only in the midst of conflict and, accordingly, they should be taken as warnings that both individual believers and the churches to which they belong may well fail in their calling. They may in fact continue to live in a way quite unworthy of that calling.

For these reasons, believers are urged to "put off" an old form of life that is characteristic of disunity and so contrary to God's secret. This old form of life, characteristic of life apart from Christ but still lingering within the life of believers, is one in which the mind has not been illumined by truth, by the revelation of God's secret purpose. In this form of life, the mind is given to "emptiness" *(mataiotēs)*. Such a mind has been darkened *(skotoomai)* and so alienated from the life of God (Eph. 4:17-18). People whose minds are in such a state have become hard of heart and so callous *(apalgeō)*. In this state they give themselves to various forms of outrageous, lewd conduct *(aselgeia)*, and all sorts of impure behavior *(akatharsia)* (Eph. 4.19). Their lives are also full of bitterness *(pikria)*, violent emotions of mind and spirit *(thumos)*, and anger *(orgē)*, all of which may be accompanied with malice *(kakia)* (Eph. 4:31).

These are the characteristics to which the life of the church is to provide a contrast. They may be expected wherever people (be they Jew or Gentile) have not been joined by faith to Christ. The author of the letter is more than aware, however, that they may appear also among believers. Believers are, therefore, strongly urged to guard against their appearance because of the particular witness it is the calling of the church to bear. Indeed, they are called to struggle with all the vigor God's grace provides against this form of life so that a life worthy of God's calling will become plain for all to see.[20]

20. Ephesians 6:10-18.

Some Conclusions

Now, to return to the place we began, one can safely say both that evangelization and, perhaps even more, re-evangelization involve something more like a gladiatorial contest *(agōn)* than a conversation, and that this contest involves more than words. The calling of the church and of each believer is to yoke the word of the cross to the way of the cross, not as a means of salvation (for we are saved by grace through faith [Eph. 2:8]) but as a necessary way of confronting the world (be it modern, pre-modern, or postmodern), exposing its true character and making manifest God's true purposes for humankind.

To put the matter another way, the first focus of Christian ethics is not, as liberals now would have it, the transformation of social order, nor is it, as those of a more evangelical temper hold, the sanctification of the individual soul. If one places the Christian life within the context of God's providence and the calling of the church, the primary focus of Christian ethics becomes the common life of the church in the midst of which believers learn a new way of life and through which they manifest an alternative reality to the "world" whose mind is given not to truth but to "emptiness."

The first step of "re-evangelization" in a postmodern world involves not only the proclamation of God's secret made known in Christ but also the presence within the body of the church of a way of life that runs counter to the "decentered" and so finally empty mind of the postmodern era. It is a way of life embedded in a coherent narrative that lays claim to truth. It is a way of life comprised of that truth, and it is a way of life that, by contrast, exposes the mind of the time as empty and its way of life as "unfruitful" and sadly dark (Eph. 5:11).

Ethics as "ecclesial" play a decisive role in the first step of re-evangelization (proclamation), but they also play a crucial role in the other aspects of the process Professor Abraham has adumbrated. That process, in addition to proclamation, involves inclusion in the church, owning certain intellectual claims, appropriation of a moral vision, recognition of and sharing in certain gifts and capacities, and finally the acceptance of forms of individual and corporate discipline. Evangelization, in short, includes within its scope *paradosis,* at least in its basic forms, and my contention is that Christian ethics, not as an academic discipline but as a form of life lived, are as essential to each aspect of this process as is what may be communicated by what, with tongue in cheek, I have called "talking heads."

Here are two examples of what I mean. It might seem that "owning a certain intellectual content" is an aspect of evangelization that lies far indeed from the realm of ethics. But is this so? The early fathers of the church to a person insisted that the knowledge of God could not be separated from living a holy life. In their minds, theology and ethics were not two separate disciplines. Ethics were as much a part of theology as were characterizations of relations between the persons of the Trinity or the two natures of Christ. Indeed, they insisted that these mysteries could not possibly be plumbed apart from living a certain form of life — one that reflected the life of Christ and so also the life of God. For them, the command found in Ephesians 5:1 to be imitators of God and so of Christ was a prerequisite for a genuine grasp of the intellectual content of Christian belief. Theology referred not to an academic discipline but to the knowledge of God, and such knowledge did not come apart from a way of life.

Or again, can recognition of and participation in certain gifts and capacities be had apart from what we call Christian ethics? What Professor Abraham has in mind when he speaks of the recognition of certain gifts are gifts of the Spirit that can be expected in the life of each believer and within the common life of the church. Evangelization requires that one be "at home" with these things, but why on earth should being at home with the gifts of the Spirit be linked to Christian ethics? It is little noted, but nonetheless true, that the discussion of spiritual gifts that occurs in the Epistle to the Ephesians occurs only after the author has spoken of the basic shape of a worthy life, only after he has spoken of those powers of soul he calls "humility of mind," "respectfulness to others as if they were one's betters," "patience," "forbearance," and a firm bent "to be eager" to maintain the unity of the church (Eph. 4:1-3). The gifts we are to expect and learn to feel at home with, he goes on to say, are intended to help the church grow up to the stature of Christ, to grow to resemble him. The implication of the passage, however, is that if the powers of soul and practices that define a worthy life are not present within the common life of the church, the gifts may be used for other purposes — purposes contrary to God's providential ordering of all things. Should this happen, the gifts would become sources of disunity rather than unity and, perhaps, no gifts at all.

And finally, to tie this discussion of Christian ethics back into what was said about "owning a certain intellectual content," our author ends his famous discussion of gifts by saying that the powers of soul and practices he has deemed worthy of the calling of the church also are necessary if the truth is to be spoken *in love* to an erring brother or sister who is apt, if the letter's wording is to be credited, to be a child or, in other words, a new convert (Eph. 4:13-16). Thus, living the Christian life would appear in this author's mind to be central not only to the proper understanding and exercise of the gifts that may be expected within the common life of the church but also to grasping in an adequate manner the truth contained in its proclamation of God's secret.

I am painfully aware that I have done no more than give the briefest outline of the central role Christian ethics play in the process of evangelization. In a postmodern world, they provide a counter-example that confronts a social world in which truth is plural and so no more than truth to someone or to some group. It is my belief that apart from this attempt to imitate God, the truth about God that Christians have to proclaim will be no more than the noise made by "talking heads." No real confrontation will take place between truth as God makes it known and truth as we would have it. Of course, even if the churches were to make the effort of re-evangelization not only by speaking the word of the cross but also by living the way of the cross, there is no guarantee that the confrontation would produce conversion and amendment of life. There is no divinely given guarantee that even our best efforts at re-evangelization will bear fruit. The haunting words of Hendrik Kraemer ought never to be forgotten lest we turn God's work of evangelization into our own: "We have," he said, "to make the observation that it is in relation to the communication of the Christian message *only* [emphasis added] that the mysterious thing happens: communication as a means of annihilation." The most faithful communication of the Christian message may well find only impenetrable hearts and so bring fearful judgment. It is the fact of what Kraemer called "cardiosclerosis" that makes evangelization and re-evangelization more like contests than conversations and it is the fact of "cardiosclerosis" that requires us to place the results of those contests in the hands of God rather than our own.

This word about God's sovereignty is always the last to be spoken whenever we speak of evangelization and particularly of the place of ethics within that process. However, given the fact that we are denizens of a postmodern world, there are a couple of penultimate words that seem appropriate. In a world that is properly "postmodern" there is at best "my truth" and "your truth," "your way of life" and "my way of life." The mind of a postmodern world does not see matters of life and death in differences of opinion but only the (bad) possibility of insisting upon one's own way or of being misunderstood. Thus, we cry for an exchange of views rather than a confrontation. I cannot speak for all the denominations for I am not privy to their inner life, but I do know that the mind of my own church is thoroughly "postmodern," and that as long as that mind presides "re evangelization" will not even be attempted. No reason for making the effort will be found beyond gaining a few more friends who think and live as you do. Nothing of life-or-death importance will be seen to be at stake.

The second penultimate word is that, should re-evangelization in the way in which I have spoken of it be undertaken as a venture of faith, that undertaking would involve a reconception and reordering of the life of the congregations of our churches. We would be forced to constitute ourselves as counterexamples of both a way of thinking and a way of living. The way of thinking to which we would have to oppose ourselves is one that, in the words of Frank Kermode, has no "sense of an ending." It is characterized only by narratives that can always be deconstructed in ways that allow their constituent elements, as in Hesse's *The Glass Bead Game,* to be arranged and rearranged in endless patterns and combinations, some more interesting than others. In this world, the way of living coheres with the way of thinking. In it one sets out on a journey to find one's own particular way — a way that coheres with one's own particular truth. The thought that truth is defined by the nature and purposes of God and that it requires one to enter a way that God has "prepared for us to walk in" (Eph. 2:10) is simply offensive. In this world, the congregation tends to define its place not as a counterexample but as a haven of affirmation where what one thinks and where one's particular way are given support and understanding. Given this fact, the most immediate question raised by "re-evangelization in the postmodern world" is whether the churches have either the vision or the strength to reorder their common life in a way that provides a living alternative to that world.

I have now made my basic points, but, before closing, allow me a postscript that explains a point made earlier. I wonder how many noted that the assigned title is "Re-evangelization *in* a Postmodern World," not "Re-evangelization *of* a Postmodern World"? Again, I must admit to a lack of knowledge of the planners' intentions, but it entered my mind that the use of the preposition "in" rather than "of" might well be an intentional act whose purpose is to make clear that "re-evangelism" in our present circumstances has neither the aim nor the likelihood of re-establishing a Christian society. Rather, its purpose is less high flying, but more realistic: namely, regardless of the consequences, to present in as faithful and direct a way possible a witness to the truth of God in Christ in the midst of a society whose fundamental presuppositions and ways of life, despite their traces of a Christian past, run counter to both the truth about God's purposes revealed in Christ Jesus and the way of life worthy of those purposes.

Given the theological fact that "cardiosclerosis" is a disease endemic to humankind and given the more immediate sociological fact that individualism is a part of the "sociologic" of our age, and given the ecclesial fact that the inner life of the churches imitates more closely the individualism of the age than the life of God, it seems unlikely that even our best efforts at "re-evangelization" carry the promise of recapturing a culture. For this reason alone, it is important to speak about re-evangelization *in* rather than re-evangelization *of* the postmodern world. In the end, it is only a matter of tactics, but it is nonetheless important to speak in this way precisely because using the preposition *in* rather than *of* signals a different agenda than that of either contemporary liberal Protestantism or its alter ego, that brand of evangelicalism known as "the Christian right." In very different ways, each of these has linked "re-evangelization" and Christian ethics with a cultural project, namely, the re-Christianization *of* American society. I have often thought that, beneath their differences, these rather strange bedfellows have a common goal — the re-establishment of a Christian America in which the churches have the assigned role of keeper of the nation's conscience. I have often thought as well that they hate each other so because, though they have a common goal, they have very divergent views about what a Christian America ought to look like. In both instances, however, "re-evangelization" and Christian ethics have a very inner-worldly goal, namely, a particular sort of social order. Both liberals and members of the Christian right, therefore, might well prefer to speak of "Re-evangelization *of* a Postmodern World," and both might see Christian ethics as central to that project.

Despite the announced death of "Constantinianism" the churches of America in all their forms continue, as churches, to pursue their "cultural mission." Nevertheless, to this observer, it appears that such a mission is both misconceived and beyond reach. In all respects, the churches are in pursuit of a chimera. For the moment, the churches are far too weak to undertake such a project, even if rightly conceived. In the end it is both more obedient and more realistic to stick with the title "Re-evangelization *in* a Postmodern World" than it is to take on the re-evangelization *of* such a world. The former project is culturally less ambitious than the latter. It is, nevertheless, more in keeping with the possibilities actually present within a postmodern world, with the freedom of the Spirit to blow where it will, and with the fundamental calling of the church in every age — namely, to bear faithful witness and leave the rest to God.

Hearts No Longer Restless: The Reawakening of Faith in the Postmodern West

ANTHONY UGOLNIK

My perspective on the issue of re-evangelization and the understanding of the Word reflects my experience in eastern Europe. I was privileged to witness and indeed take a modest role in the reawakening of my faith tradition on its Russian and Ukrainian soil. There is a uniqueness to most human situations, but the scale and rapidity with which the Orthodox faith, once repressed and subjected to strict legal controls, grew and reclaimed its place among what we might call a "de-evangelized" people are surely unprecedented.

Making analogies between one people and another is dangerous. Yet as a literary scholar with an American cultural identity and as a priest in an East European religious tradition, I can at least comment with some attention to comparisons.

There is no real consensus about the status of religion in public life in the United States. Some observers, myself among them, have very recently deplored the marginalization of religion in political and intellectual life. Scholars of religion like George Marsden in *The Soul of the American University* (1994) and scholars of government like Stephen Carter in *The Culture of Disbelief* (1993) have earned a broad hearing on the same thesis within the last decade. A new breeze may be stirring, but what it stirs is as yet unclear. The academy retains its marks of segregation between religious and secular constituencies. Public discourse, however, has undergone a shift in both Russia and the United States. George Bush and Joe Lieberman both integrated references to their religious commitments in the course of the last U.S. presidential campaign. Vladimir Putin in Russia attends Patriarchal liturgies as a head of state and discusses a dawning spiritual awareness. The heads of state in both Ukraine and Belarus involve the government in consolidating and promoting religious life, sometimes in partisan ways.

The "Strange New Word of the Gospel," then, emerges in both our countries in strange new contexts. It is possible for intellectuals to encounter the gospel as if for the first time, after having been insulated from it and after having received only an idea of what it contains from those who do not confess it. It is also possible in both East and West for believing people to hear a privatized version of the Word, which they may not quite recognize, promoted in a public context. "Re-evangelization," then, has to take not only the Word but also its audience into account.

"Re-evangelization" is a term that itself requires some unpacking. If evangelization indicates that the gospel has been imparted, then the prefix implies that the process has been repeated. What is not quite clear, and perhaps too easily assumed, is that the gospel has been received in the same way under both conditions. Yet what we know of culture and the nature of language itself teaches us quite clearly that just as words themselves are subject to a process of drift and change, so also are the contexts within which words are received.

This attention to context and audience is something that East Europeans, even at the popular level, may apprehend as a function of their culture. Seminal Christian Orthodox apologists like Alexei Khomiakov (1804-1860), and also writers with a manifest Orthodox identity like Nikolai Gogol (1809-1852) and Fyodor Dostoëvsky (1821-1881), were ready to see the medium of the faith as primarily cultural. Ethnicity was not a prefix to the faith (Russian or Greek Orthodox) because any particular ethnicity was the sole vehicle to the gospel. Rather, one's language and culture were seen to be a necessary adjunct to evangelization itself. "Preach to all nations" is an injunction in which the collective object is taken seriously.

That element of collectivity extends itself to the realm of contemporary Orthodox hermeneutics and interpretation. It is as peoples that the principle of *sobornost* or conciliarity is deployed among Orthodox in their own understanding. Papal authority is rejected in the East not because it is authoritative, but rather because it emerges from a single voice; it is seen as an emblem for the western construct of the intellect itself. Indeed, Orthodox critiques of western thinkers from Augustine to Barth tend to view the tension between rationalism and mystery as an emblem of the distinction between the single interpretative mind asserting the truth of the gospel, and the collective mind of a people expressing the gospel's transformative power. Protestantism in that view is a mutation of Catholicism; both employ a similar vector in the expression of truth.

It can be argued that the nature of truth itself takes on what Westerners might see as a relative tone in the East, and this long before the postmodern, "post-Christian" era. The Russian émigré theologian Georges Florovsky (1893-1979) asserted that "Scripture is the icon of truth," rather than truth itself.[1] He uses the word *eikon* with two modes of resonance: given the Eastern sensitivity to the image as a conveyance of the Word, Scripture is an "envisioning" of truth, at least symbolically suggested by the image-studded encasement in which the gospel is clad and borne in procession at any Orthodox ritual. Second, Florovsky is also profoundly aware of variations among languages and their effect upon understanding and consciousness. His theological elder Sergius Bulgakov (1879-1944) viewed the polyglot state of God's people as an emblem of the Fall, and saw in dialogic conciliarity an opportunity to ameliorate its effects. Florovsky saw Scripture in its varied linguistic incarnations as an approximation, partitive at that, of a truth that was manifest in the text but at the same time separate from it. Orthodox would join the postmodern linguists in asserting the impossibility of "literal truth." Indeed, they would go so far as to call the very idea a modernist heresy.

"Re-evangelization," then, in this view would take on the nature of a "re-imaging." The signifier, or rather the word, is an arbitrary thing in linguistic terms. When words are reawakened, or put to new uses in reawakening the gospel among a people, they distance themselves of necessity from their old significance. The "icon" of truth changes. Indeed, to some extent the understanding of that truth changes. The postmodern gospel, in that sense, must rescue the Word from that former significance which time and hence triteness have destroyed.

---

1. Georges Florovsky, *Bible, Church, Tradition* (Belmont, Mass.: Nordland, 1972), p. 48.

I say this to assert some affinity between the Orthodox mistrust of empirical rationalism and the postmodern mind. In its relentless critique of absolute categories, indeed of the capacity to convey an idea from one mind to another with utter confidence as to meaning, there is a hospitality between the Orthodox mind and the postmoderns who challenge the very concept of Orthodoxy.

The Russian formalists shaped a school of literary criticism sometimes called "the last of the Soviet avant-garde." Their theory was focused upon the nature of poetry and literary language, and in its approach it illustrates more than hints of an affinity with the Slavic religious mind. The formalists rejected the idea that the genius of creative narrative shone forth in its ability to convey received wisdom, or to impart the static beauty of a language much like what Keats captured in his Grecian urn. Rather, the formalists saw the essential function of poetic language as resting in its ability to destabilize and upset the phenomenon of meaning. What a successful poem or image achieved was not to capture an idea, but rather to see it anew, to "de-familiarize" it, to rescue it from the triteness and appropriation of daily language, a triteness that freezes and petrifies meaning with its cliché and banality.

Viktor Shklovskii saw not only the poet, but also the reader and interpreter as involved in this process of rescue. Whereas the artist re-awakens language by creating new forms of language for old ones, the reader and interpreter also do so by recycling those old forms through a de-familiarizing re-creation of them. Shklovskii, for example, complained that Russia was losing its grasp of its own master poet: "We are losing the living perception of Pushkin not because our thought and language are far removed from his, but because we did not change the standard to which we compare him."[2] The language of the gospel is parallel to that of any text. What interpreters must do, as the very sense of words tends to fade and die around them, is continually re-create the correspondences and standards for those words that they might take on life once more.

De-familiarization is different from re-familiarization, to be sure. But there is a wisdom in viewing the power of the gospel in this sense as that of a hyperpoetic text. Jesus takes on the received wisdom of the

---

2. "Evgenii Onegin: Pushkin I Stern," *Ocerki po poetike Pushkina* (Berlin, 1923), p. 220.

Law and the Prophets, yet his use of its terms is to allow us to recon-
struct them, even deconstruct them. The device of the parables, with
the very challenge that accompanies them — their resistance to common understanding — demands a "de-familiarization" of the common
terms of religious understanding. "This is why I speak to them in parables, because seeing they do not see, and hearing they do not hear,
nor do they understand" (Matt. 13:13). Jesus also employs poetic language and rich metaphor, and in so doing he "de-familiarizes" the assumptions of his audience.

The author and literary critic J. R. R. Tolkien saw his own art, and
that of the folktales and "faery stories" as he called them, as essentially the rescue of words from triteness. In a fable that represented
trees as giants talking in low, resounding tones, or walking with
rootlike toes grasping the earth, he hoped we would never see a tree in
quite the same terms again. By the same token, he saw the gospel as
containing the greatest possibility in this act of profound rescue:

> This story begins and ends in joy. It has preeminently the "inner con-
> sistency of reality." There is no tale ever told that men would rather
> find was true, and none which so many skeptical men have accepted
> as true on its own merits. For the Art of it has the supremely convinc-
> ing tone of Primary Art, that is, of Creation. To reject it leads either to
> sadness or to wrath.[3]

This sense of fresh and new apprehension is always eluding us.
The terms of discourse in which the world receives the gospel is at
continual and paradoxical war with the way the gospel demands to be
understood. If the gospel is received, appropriated, and integrated
into the culture and language of a people, then it becomes "familiar-
ized." It becomes in effect trite. Those of us who receive and believe
the gospel perceive that triteness in our own reception of the Word.
Monastic texts enjoin those who meditate upon the Word to "attend
to it," see it afresh. Liturgical ritual repeatedly commands us to "attend" (prosechōmen), to not only hear but to overcome our resistance to
hearing. We Orthodox tend to see conversion as a social, even a cosmic process. When we speak of evangelization as we do today, not
only as an individual but also as a social or cultural process, the chal-

---

3. J. R. R. Tolkien, "On Faery Stories," *The Monsters and the Critics and Other Essays*
(Boston: Houghton Mifflin, 1984), p. 156.

lenge to that triteness also becomes a social injunction. We must look for the connection between re-evangelization and de-familiarization. We are asked not so much to preach the gospel anew, but rather to rescue the gospel from those meanings and significances to which others and even we ourselves have put it in our most somnolent moments.

Postmodern texts often assume that religious assent is an anachronistic act. Postmodern understanding, whatever that is (and it is confessed to be a fluid thing indeed), is sure of the fact that it excludes an assumed or common understanding. As one of my colleagues unpacked a common phrase in one of those short morning essays on National Public Radio, "I'm sure I don't know." That is the one thing of which he is sure. Belief becomes what Paul Ricoeur called "the first naïveté."

And indeed, in its campaign against religious belief, the Office of Religious Affairs in the Soviet era had a great deal in common with the American academic establishment. For it was not the challenge of the gospel which the Soviets portrayed as the object of its critique; rather, it was the appropriated understanding of the gospel. The Soviet authorities were not sure they didn't know, they were sure that there was nothing to be known. That is, the Soviets critiqued a folk religion, a naïve faith, a trite gospel, all of which seemed to them to be sure. By the same token the postmodern skepticism about claims of faith most often focuses upon the understanding of the gospel that has been appropriated, that affirms existing structures, rather than the gospel that challenges our structures themselves, even structures of thought. That is, it is the familiar gospel, and not the hyperpoetic and de-familiarizing text, which the secular mind in both cultures has rejected.

And if its critics have rejected in essence a false gospel, a gospel of frozen and unchallenged significances, the assumed truth rather than the "icon of Truth," then so also have many of those who defend the faith against those challenges. The absolutes that many defenders of the faith affirm against attack are often associated with social institutions of church and political structure. Bishop Spong deconstructs incarnation, resurrection, and even divinity. He does not, however, quite so thoroughly deconstruct the office of bishop that lends him his voice. Institutions must bear their own critique, quite apart from the gospel they appropriate and express.

The quest for the historical Jesus has discomfited, at some point or another, most of our religious traditions. My own tradition is no exception. But viewed in the light of "de-familiarization," Jesus scholarship has evolved into a phenomenon with rich possibilities for us all. The insights of my own tradition, in my opinion at least, help us to rescue the quest for a historical Jesus from its own pitfalls. The Jesus Seminar can seem to be an empirically rationalist quest for truth at odds with, but no less absolute than, any of our faith claims. All language, not just religious language, rationalist discourse and the discourse of faith, needs to be rescued from triteness. A scholarship that sees itself as debunking claims is as hostage to those claims as those who embrace them without question. The gospel rescues or de-familiarizes both sets of understanding, and replaces them with something *else*, something radically new in nature.

A quest for a historical Jesus can be no less imperial than an authoritative Christian dictate regarding Jesus, especially if we regard the question as a battle between two individual wills, or even two sets of a type of individual will. The gospel expresses itself as a struggle for Israel, a people of God. Jesus scholarship has made stirring progress in understanding the context of the Word, placing the voice of this candidate for the Meshiakh in the context of the various Judaic factions of his time. With the help of that scholarship we begin to see what Jesus of Nazareth says in the light of the hypertext: he challenges the understandings of each faction, overturning the terms in which each of them appropriates the Word. He rescues the Word from appropriation and familiarity; he "de-familiarizes" it. The result is a re-envisioning of God, a new way of seeing and apprehension. It is this process — the apprehension, and not its object as frozen in some construct of truth — that we must recapture.

I have often asked myself, as a college professor and a man of Christian faith, what is in spiritual if not in scholarly terms a pressing question. Why is it that in Russia I could attract a hall full of students willing to discuss issues of faith and culture, offered in inconvenient places and at the most inconvenient hours, whereas in the States an attempt to corral a dozen students into a like assembly is like a labor of Hercules? And the answer is not that they are lazy: as a hockey coach I could get a bus full of volunteers to play a game two hours away at midnight. The answer is a simple one on a lot of levels. Most significantly, in my opinion, the students in Russia are engaging in an act of reappropriation, a critique of former modes of understanding.

In the U.S., no words could be drearier in most circles than the juxtaposition of "Bible" and "study." Bible studies are not seen to defamiliarize anything. They are perceived to be a model for triteness.

Evangelical models in the U.S., especially the most successful ones, seem to put the lie to my assertion. Megachurches constitute a kind of Christian sprawl, and revival efforts can fill stadiums with — but the question is, with what? With individuals, who find in the gospel an answer to their personal dilemmas? With those whose quest is for a personal Jesus (a term very difficult to translate into Slavic languages without making Jesus sound like a type of toothbrush)? Jesus answers personal questions. He does not save a people, rescue a nation, transform a culture. He becomes a tranquilizer for a soul besieged.

These conversions, however liberating and therapeutic, are no more than a beginning: they are an individual rather than a cultural phenomenon. They seem to challenge, but in fact they do not. They act in reaction to the larger culture with a different set of appropriations, rather than with a transformative challenge to its sets of meaning. As one who teaches early American literature and confronts students with its texts, I would maintain that the modern evangelical phenomenon is not in the tradition of great American awakenings, but rather in the tradition of a consumerism that is the greatest triteness of them all. Jesus as object of our appetites, intellectual or spiritual, offers himself to be appropriated. Jesus as the Way, the initiation to a process whereby we transform, transfigure, and reapprehend the world, is by all means a real Awakening.

Jonathan Edwards (1703-58) is my favorite theologian (non-Orthodox, of course). He also works very well with my students, but only if I am careful to rescue him from the appropriation to which the secular academy has put him. Ironically enough, the central text by which Jonathan Edwards is known to those few classrooms that still study him is his sermon "Sinners in the Hands of an Angry God." The irony rests of course in what Jonathan Edwards himself eventually recognized: what the sermon offers is a motivation to the individual soul to submit to his greatest fears, to be in effect appropriated by the terms of the sermon. The emphasis here is not on how the believer sees God, but rather on how an imagined God sees the believer:

> The God that holds you over the pit of hell, much as one holds a spider, or some loathsome insect, over the fire, abhors you, and is dread-

fully provoked; his wrath towards you burns like fire; he looks upon you as worthy of nothing else, but to be cast into the fire; he is of purer eyes than to bear to have you in his sight; you are ten thousand times so abominable in his eyes as the most venomous serpent is in ours.[4]

The text is useful to the secular academy and those who teach about Puritanism with a sneer exactly because it is so predictable. It offers students precisely what they imagine the Puritans to have been.

Jonathan Edwards, of course, was a very late Puritan. Though he died before the Revolution, he was a rough contemporary of Jefferson and Franklin. And like the forgers of a nation, Jonathan Edwards forged an American religious imagination not by this emphasis upon surrender, but rather upon active apprehension of God in the world. And Edwards offered an avenue to that apprehension quite Orthodox even in our terms when he focused, at length and in some of his most brilliant work, upon that softest of topics especially in current religious scholarship: beauty. Beauty was to Edwards, as it was to Nevin in the Mercersburg school of theology, a central theological category because in its apprehension lay a reappropriation of the understanding.

That mixture of all sorts of rays, which we call white, is a proportionate mixture that is harmonious (as Sir Isaac Newton has shown) to each particular simple color and contains in itself some harmony or other that is delightful. And each sort of ray plays a distinct tune to the soul, besides those lovely combinations that are found in nature — those ineffable beauties in the green face of the earth, in all manner of flowers, in the color of the skies, in the lovely tinctures of the morning and the evening.[5]

The believer in apprehending beauty actively reconstructs and reenvisions the redemption of his or her world. The apprehension of beauty in effect rescues the world from sterile constructs of language and the triteness of conveyed meaning. This is a gospel open to the imagination, a gospel manifest in what is beautiful in culture. This is a gospel that can resonate with the arts.

It is in this neglected dimension of the American religious imagi-

---

4. Jonathan Edwards, "Sinners in the Hands of an Angry God," *Jonathan Edwards Reader*, ed. John E. Smith et al. (New Haven: Yale University Press, 1995), p. 98.

5. Jonathan Edwards, "The Beauty of the World," *Jonathan Edwards Reader*, p. 15.

nation, its hospitality to beauty, that we find a common possibility for the American and Slavic encounters with the postmodern. The gospel as a hyperpoetic text "de-familiarizes" our own apprehensions of the gospel and allows us to see it and the world anew.

Edwards initiated the first of many American religious awakenings. Russian counterparts to that same process of "awakening" also tended to emphasize Beauty and the immanence of God in the world. The seat of that awareness, in this collectively envisioned culture, is in the heart. Pamphil Yurkevich (1826-1874), the Ukrainian theologian and tutor of the more widely known Solovyev, is the one who provided an Orthodox philosophical synthesis for the "prayer of the heart." Yurkevich was influential in the Slavic religious renaissance of the nineteenth century, and he shifted the terms of the monastic hesychast method of prayer into the realm of hermeneutics and understanding. Exploring his era's understanding of the physiological contrast between the brain and the heart, Yurkevich rejects the idea "that thinking is the very essence of the soul, that is, that thinking composes the whole spiritual man."[6]

Yurkevich does not reject in any sense the rational impulse, but rather insists that the gospel demands a harmony between the mind's thought and the heart's empathy. Nor, in Orthodox terms at least, does faith bring rest to the mind. Vladimir Lossky speaks of a "crucified mind" in encounter with the Trinity. The gospel can, however, bring its peace to the heart and the fulfillment of our empathetic impulse in loving relationship. The soul's encounter with the gospel is not a purely intellectual apprehension, but what we might call a "heart's understanding." In fact, the phenomenon of the heart's understanding is more akin to an empathy implicit in the process of the arts rather than an act of intellection born in the process of rational thought.

This is the sense in which Yurkevich anticipates most Slavic thinkers. Yet he rejects the terms of western rationalism and hence the primacy of individual, rational judgment, but only when it is employed in the absence of an "empathetic balance." The emphasis upon empathy rather than rational understanding placed that very a-rational process, the process of love, at the service not only of the individual but also of

---

6. Pamphil Yurkevich, *Tvori [Works]*, ed. Stephan Jarmus (Winnipeg: St. Andrews College, 1979), p. 97.

the society in which he was placed. Empathy, especially with suffering, must be not only individually but socially expressed in the church and in the broader society.

Monasteries have not only a religious but also a social function to the Orthodox mind because they are as institutions leavens of the culture. By the same token, the believer whose heart is attuned to God can act as a social leaven and cause others to see the image, to apprehend the beauty they have neglected.

The Ukrainian author Nikolai Gogol presents us with the specter of a radical "de-familiarization" in his literary satire. Those who appropriate and reflect the received social meanings distort and disfigure the image of God in creation. By the same token, in his commentary on the liturgy itself, Gogol shows us that those who worship God undergo a capacity to apprehend a formerly hidden beauty in the world. Worship becomes a social act. They go forth from the liturgy enriched and socially empowered to effect that beauty around them. After leaving the temple in which they have attended the divine love feast, they look upon all people as brothers and sisters. Whether they resume their customary tasks in business or in the family, or wherever they may be, they involuntarily preserve in their souls the high resolve of such association with others as is inspired by the love brought from heaven by the God-Man.[7]

Dostoëvsky, like Gogol, has a profound theological resonance in Orthodox circles. Similarly, Dostoëvsky's spiritually enlightened characters recognize a profound beauty, and share that recognition in places where beauty is seldom seen as manifest. Thus the Idiot bows down before the image of Christ he perceives in a beggar or a prostitute.

The sharp distinction between intellectual and spiritual empowerment resides precisely in the renunciation of power, prestige, and honor as categories. The tendency to academicize religion and make theology a matter of intellect is a constant refrain of critique in Orthodox sources. This mistrust of academic perception has its parallels in postmodern theorists. Both critique the power of the intellect to fully grasp meaning. Saints like Seraphim, rather than theologians like Yurkevich, are seen to be the figures who apprehend, rather than

---

7. Nikolai Gogol, *Meditations on the Divine Liturgy* (Jordanville, N.Y.: Holy Trinity Monastery Press, n.d.), p. 57.

those who understand the process of apprehension. (Saints in our tradition seldom write papers like this one.)

The methods of "de-familiarization" for the Russians of the nineteenth and earliest twentieth century were to estrange the church from the power and prestige that many of its main figures endorsed. The poor, the discredited, the rejected became in fact the very ones who apprehended the beauty in God and the meaning of his gospel. They did so by evoking and sustaining the capacity of empathy, the capacity of the human heart, and by deriving an Orthodox identity from the community in which they lived.

The three major figures I see in the Soviet reawakening of the faith, the ones who prepared the ground for the subsequent reclaiming of the faith, were Pavel Florensky, Mikhail Bakhtin, and Alexander Men. Each of them, in his own way, developed this idea of "de-familiarization" of the terms in which the faith was previously understood. Each of them was also instrumental in drawing a generation of people to the faith in the face of the most pervasive, concentrated, and threatening "de-evangelization" of the past century. Each of them embodies three ideas. First, there is an *embedded gospel*, ready to be uncovered in any people at any time. Second, there is *a dialogic gospel*, which no one of us is capable of articulating, but the understanding of which is dependent on our listening to the nature of that "embedded gospel" in each other. And third, there is the concept of an *immanent gospel*, which can draw from the arts of a people even when its texts are suppressed. Thus first apprehended in the arts, it can emerge triumphant through its persecuted or quiescent phase to reclaim a people who are educated into receiving it.

First, Pavel Florensky (1882-1937) is a figure whose work has only recently been translated into English. A scientist as well as a priest-theologian, he was a figure in the Russian religious renaissance of the last century. Drawn into a serious connection with the Orthodox faith before the Russian revolution, he was ordained a priest just before the onset of the Bolshevik terror. His masterwork, *The Pillar and Ground of Truth*, was published in St. Petersburg in 1914, and copies of it were cherished and preserved through the Soviet years among believers and seminarians.

First of all, Florensky was multidisciplinary, a scientist and mathematician, fully conversant with the vocabulary and methodology of empirical rationalism. Yet his great work on the nature of the Christian faith, while it freely uses the terms of scientific rationalism, uses them in such a way that they become an indication of and a metaphor for the spiritual quest for identity. One of Florensky's primary theses is that identity can never be discovered within the autonomous mind. The entity "A" emerges as "A" only in comparison with that which is *not* "A." Thus identity is born in difference, even in that mystery which separates me from all that is not understood. His quest for the phenomenon of identity, relentless and far-reaching anthropologically, is a profoundly postmodern one. What one finds in his pages is the detailed development of a theodicy, a teaching about God, which is present and implicit in virtually all ages and at all times.

Just as "not A" is necessary to "A"'s existence, so also doubt is necessary to faith. Doubt, that accompaniment to postmodern existence, is an accompaniment to his thought and a constituent of identity. The relationship of doubt to the mind of the consistent skeptic is one that Florensky describes with the wrenching familiarity of one who has been there.

In the same way that an object is accompanied by a shadow, every affirmation is accompanied by the excruciating desire for the opposite affirmation. After having inwardly said "yes" to ourselves, we say "no" at the same moment. But the earlier "no" longs for "yes." "Yes" and "no" are inseparable. Doubt, in the sense of uncertainty, is far away. Absolute doubt has now begun, doubt as the total impossibility of affirming anything at all, even its own non-affirmation. Pressing stage by stage, manifesting the idea that inheres in *nuce*, skepticism reaches its own negation but cannot leap across that negation. And so it becomes an infinitely excruciating torment, an agony of the spirit.[8]

Trinity, identity in community, is an ultimate answer to the skeptic's dilemma. Freed by a loving anthropology, kinship with all others, one is also freed from the enclosing autonomy of the intellect. Florensky searches through the images and emblems and archetypes of successive civilizations and ages to see in them the seeds or foreshadowings of the trinitarian doctrines to come. Florensky sees in pre-Christian civilization not a gnostic key to meaning, but rather what I would call a "mythic longing" for the fulfillment of the gospel. We see in him an attempt to prove what Tolkien asserted: "There is no

8. Pavel Florensky, *The Pillar and Ground of Truth*, trans. Boris Jakim (Princeton: Princeton University Press, 1997), p. 29.

tale ever told that men would rather find was true. . . ." In Florensky, that ardent wish emerges in the mythic and anthropological records of human civilization. In the record of our mythology rests the evidence and the nature of our longing. Florensky studies the common structures of those myths and even the structure of our mathematics to explore the nature — even the imperative — of our longing. Ultimately he seeks to demonstrate the way in which our Christian doctrine answers the precise nature of what it is we long for.

The attraction of an anthropological methodology with openness to scientific and mathematical terms to a secular Soviet culture is clear. The Soviet academy suppressed the gospel so completely that Passolini's film, "The Gospel of St. Matthew," was the first Gospel that the neo-Christian activists of the late seventies, who were imprisoned for their faith, had actually witnessed. The study of religious anthropology, however, was admitted — if only as a curiosity. Florensky did not go into western exile. On his home soil, suffering the same fate as his audience, he gave those within the Soviet system a way to take that religious mythography, from the Yakut peoples of the Siberian north to the classical myths of Homer's Hellespont, and make of it the promise of the gospel repressed in their own midst.

Florensky took the Orthodox emphasis on Trinity and made of it not only a model of human interaction and love, but also a model of consciousness. The Trinity in its person was, as he developed it, the very model of human identity. As first developed by the Cappadocian Fathers and further elaborated through such Byzantine figures as Joseph Byrenios, in this conception each person of the Trinity is integral and yet implicit in its interlocutors. Each person of the Trinity is reciprocally defined in the other. Florensky saw the nature of the human personality, demonstrated in actions of love, as a reflection, however pale, of that trinitarian nature. He saw, with most Slavic thinkers, consciousness itself as a communal phenomenon: as the Slavic languages phrase the term, *soznanie*, "a knowing-together." Just as there is procession among persons of the Trinity, each of us, he taught, in some way processes from the other. Each of us in loving relationship can become "co-substantial" with the other. What is significant is that he saw this as a development of the nature of human relationship, evident and perhaps perfected in the gospel but not given its full intellectual expression.

Finally, Florensky took the artistic evidence everywhere evident in

pre-Soviet Slavic culture and held up in its most precious monument
— iconography — and made of that also an emblem of the human condition. Each of us is made in the image of God. Orthodox iconography
is a testimony to incarnation: that which can be enfleshed can also be
portrayed. Yet it is the methodology of the iconographer, from its earliest periods, to transfigure the flesh in such a way as to see its divine
immanence. Thus the conventions of iconography — the attenuation
of the limbs and the expression of the physiognomy — are evidence
not of our innate spiritual nature, but rather of the immanence of the
Spirit which is present in the flesh. That same immanence, the "coming to be" of the image of God in us, is present also in the icon of our
own bodily incarnation. Each of us, in body and in physiognomy, is
"theosis" in process, a "coming unto the Divine." Florensky takes an
attitude toward embodiment that defies the critique of Christianity
applied by western scholars such as Margaret Miles, who take as an
item of dogma that Christianity somehow denigrates and even disfig-
ures the body. The human icon, as Florensky develops it, is a testimony to our dignity as those in whom the Spirit takes its indwelling.

This attitude toward iconography, and of course toward the
beauty that is the ultimate standard of the icon's fidelity to the idea of
its Creator, defies the functional standard of beauty that pervades the
secular mind. For beauty that resides in function and utility to the
means of production, present in the Socialist era, undoes the model of
the body as that which is faithful to its ultimate model in Christ. The
category of beauty, then, as the expression of a harmony among all rational elements, conflicted with the dialectic implicit in Soviet Marx-
ism, which demanded an eternal conflict between synthesis and antithesis. It was the articulation of beauty as a theological category that
made Florensky so enduring a figure through the darkest days of Soviet persecution. The records of theses written at the Theological
Academy in St. Petersburg, then Leningrad, show the pervasive influence of this figure, barely known in the West, as a light unto those
who remained faithful to Orthodoxy during the time of its trials. Most
significantly, he is important to the formation of those who "re-
evangelized" Russia and the Ukraine when the persecution was lifted.

Florensky remained a priest to the end of his life and died in the
Gulag. One of his associates in the Russian religious renaissance,
however, eventually became a literary critic with marginal acceptabil-
ity and publication in the Soviet environment, and still receives en-

SYNTHESIS   ONE   UNITY
ANTITHESIS   MANY   DIVERSITY

thusiastic reception in the secular American academy. If Florensky is tainted in any sense with the category of idealism, Mikhail Bakhtin (1895-1975) has unmistakable postmodern credentials. The degree to which he remained Orthodox is, in the West, a matter to raise hackles. He became known here, and popularized among academics here, as a neo-Marxist critic. Since he has become in so many ways a secular icon, his religious antecedents are sometimes not raised in polite company. That, however, is his precise charm with respect to this topic. Bakhtin is in some sense the perfect "re-evangelizer" because he provides that postmodern critical credential: the subversive text.

Let us set aside the question of Bakhtin's relationship to the Orthodox Church or even Christianity. In his youth he was known to have consorted with the Russian neo-Christians and to have written on the Trinity, that archetype — in Christian terms at least — of dialogue and reciprocal definition. What needs no documentation is the vital importance of this thinker to Christian intellectuals during the long Soviet era. The dilemma of those intellectuals is similar to the situation of so many Christians who subsist in this postmodern culture, where Christian discourse is, if not repressed, then certainly confined to its own arena. Evangelization means entry into the realm of meaning set aside from the gospel. Therefore those who can in some way introduce Christian categories into secular thought, who can as it were "de-familiarize" the terms of discourse in such a way as to place them in accordance with the gospel, are the most successful of evangelists.

Bakhtin did precisely that. He introduced theological categories into the most repressive and Stalinist of environments, and he did so through literature much as Florensky had used symbolism and the visual arts. His emphasis on dialogic theory rejected the monovocal, "epic" voice of earlier narrative, and delved instead into the form of the novel and multivoiced narrative to see the phenomenon of meaning and truth emerging from a multiplicity of voices instead of one epic pronouncement. Here, in his commentary on Dostoëvsky, is the germ of his dialogic theory:

> To be means to communicate dialogically. When the dialogue is finished, all is finished. Therefore the dialogue, in essence, cannot and must not come to an end. On the level of his religious-utopian *Welt-*

anschauung Dostoëvsky carries the dialogue over into eternity, thinking of it as an eternal co-rejoicing, co-admiration, and concord. . . .
One voice alone concludes nothing or decides nothing. Two voices is
the minimum for life, for existence.[9]

So many of us imagine and construct, despite our trinitarian
roots, the voice of God as "one voice alone" issuing forth from "one
Person alone." But discourse here emerges in the interplay of many
voices, and the nature of the Word changes radically in emphasis.
Meaning is not, cannot be derived from the pronouncement of a single
authority. Rather, the emphasis is upon the exchange between the
utterer and the one to whom the word is uttered. The word is not only
spoken, it is heard. And in that act of transmission in the process of
discourse, the Word becomes as fragile, as vulnerable as does the flesh
itself in the act of incarnation. The Word belongs not only to the one
who utters it, but also in its appropriation, and in the response, it belongs as much to the one who listens and responds. Evangelization
(or "re-evangelization," which compounds even more the sense of
continuing dialogue) imparts the word in a new realm; it is shared between utterer and audience, the church and its hearers, in a new context and a new realm. And hence it can no longer belong to the same
constructs of hearing; indeed, it subsists in a new environment of exchange. There can be no transference of the old wine into new skins,
for the word subsists in its dialogic deployment.

In the concept of "carnivale," a sense of "play" implicit in the act
of dialogue itself, we can use Bakhtin to develop a new sense of the
gospel's dialogic possibilities. Contrasting earlier epic with later development of narrative in Rabelais and Chaucer, Bakhtin demonstrates how meaning is subverted and redeployed as narrative moves
toward modernity. There is no longer one epic tale; many tales emerge
in response to each other. For if dialogue shows us the growth and
malleability of meaning in discourse, once we envision the word as ut-
terance we can also see that significances, even structures can be un-
dercut, satirized, and given new meanings.

"Carnivale" refers to ritual (as in Mardi Gras and Fasching) as
much as literary meaning; for in various ritual environments, we dress
up in each other's garb, mimic each other, and mime each other. Thus

---

9. Mikhail Bakhtin, *Problems of Dostoëvsky's Poetics* (Minneapolis: University of Minnesota Press, 1986), p. 213.

each can see his or her own weaknesses exposed, and hypocrisies un-done, in the other. "De-familiarization," then, becomes not only a ver-bal but also a social process: the oppressor can see himself in the eyes of the oppressed.

Applied to the gospel, the text then becomes that poetic "hyper-text" which liberates truth from the tyranny of pronouncement and makes it instead a lived actuality, deployed in loving and dialogic rela-tionship. Jesus scholarship, begun in the quest to find the verifiable message of that historical figure, reveals instead a Jesus who exists in critique and interplay with those established traditions of his own time. Thus the gospel is liberated to become an instrument of loving exchange among those with the courage to expose the terms of power relationships, empty pomp, and false values in the world. The gospel is the genesis of "carnivale." The dialogic gospel is not comic but in fact filled with a joy that comedy only imitates. It is eucatastrophe in the literal sense — it undoes tragedy itself.

The last figure in the Soviet reawakening, Alexander Men (1935-1990) died at a time when the gospel was just emerging from the shadow of the censor. Florensky and Bakhtin had shown the church what some commentators in Soviet times called "pastoral aesthetics," the power of the church to reveal beauty through culture to those who lived within it. Men, freed of at least some of their constraints, was able as a priest and intellectual to practice that aesthetic. The gospel as the hyperpoetic text "de-familiarized" in this sense the terms of secular, censored discourse to reveal the immanence of God.

Father Men was well read in the Christian classics culled from var-ious places during a Stalinist era when they were removed from social currency. Steeped then in the tradition, he sought to make that tradi-tion manifest in every arena from which it was absent. In his public preaching, in his dialogic sermons, in his exchanges with atheist intel-lectuals, Men sought to draw from the cultural store available to all members of his society, in order to reveal the manifestation of Christ that was locked within. He attracted immediately, then, those intellec-tuals who were surprised to find in the church a dialogic forum rather than a body of propositions. He also attracted all those for whom the architecture, art, music, and literature of Russia had meaning — in short, all those who were a part of his own people.

Russians who were active in the religious reawakening found in Father Men — particularly in his book *The Son of Man* and in his sermons — a vital, engaged figure. The organization in St. Petersburg with which I worked in the late 1980s and early 1990s, the Society for an Open Christianity, received inspiration from him. Nowadays various organizations, a university, and a movement bear his name in Russia. He is the inspiration for a new school of catechesis that engages all, believers and nonbelievers alike, in a dialogue that reflects after all an inner dialogue within each of us.

Opposed to this movement, however, and critical of Father Men in the darkest of ways, are those who attack him as representative of a "Jewish," even "Masonic" influence in the church. For these partisans — and their anti-Semitism is of a piece with their appetite for repression — Father Men is the antithesis to the monovocal, authoritarian voice of the church, whose primary function is to speak without the expectation of dialogue or response — only obedience, conformity, and submission. In their eyes Men represents the postmodern poison in the church, and it is this very spirit that martyred him in the most Russian of ways, an ax driven through the skull on a winter's day in 1990. "De-familiarization" is a dangerous concept to them indeed; and the idea of "carnivale" or subverted meaning more dangerous still. The mantle of oppression has passed from the epaulets of the Soviet State to the shoulders of these hyper-Orthodox people.

This neofascist strain in the Russian church is so often seen as a phenomenon particular to them. Yet I want to emphasize that Father Men was profoundly Orthodox in the dogma he professed; he saw the manifestation of that dogma, its immanence, in the larger culture. He was open then, as were Florensky and Bakhtin, to all those willing to engage it, just as all Orthodox must be willing to engage the voices of those far removed from us in identity. Our very engagement reciprocally defines us: Orthodoxy itself is the product of challenges to its tenets and communal engagement with its definition. Without Arius there would be no Nicea.

What we must find in our postmodern environment is the arena to deploy that dialogue when religious discourse endures in effect a kind of intellectual apartheid. One of the fundamental reactions of postmodernism is to the gospel as pronouncement, the church as "authority" in a tyrannical sense. A new evangelism can exploit that reaction by rejecting the "epic" and monovocal sense of the gospel and releasing it into the realm of the Word's dialogic engagement with us in our quest for meaning. One of the most fruitful, vital, and productive senses in which that can be done is in one of the most neglected realms within the American church — the arts. For the arts in the act of searching for meaning have largely been surrendered to the secular world, the popular media, and the academy. The culture of theology among us by and large privileges the mind and exiles that entity visible to us Orthodox as the heart; in our effort to demonstrate a toughness of mind we categorize the arts as "soft." We confine our efforts to academic structures that reflect, and at times beg to participate in, the processes of the worldly Academy. Serious interpretation and the quest for meaning are primarily an intellectual, philosophical, empirical enterprise. We build systems. The terminology alone testifies to our enclosure.

As a member of the Christians in the Visual Arts, I can testify to the frustration of Christian artists in our midst. Arts are an adjunct to our enterprise, not a medium for our expression. Even the forms of the arts that the church commissions tend to be specific, historically bound, even didactic. The church long ago abandoned the extent of its role as patron and sponsor of the arts in exchange for the intellectual academy, an academy that has divorced itself from us. There are some attempts to remedy the problem, but they are confined to an imitation of the popular culture. The efforts among one segment of us — ironically enough, the evangelicals derived from the most iconoclastic of traditions — confine the arts to a set of popular, "alternative" genres: Christian rock, Christian romances, Christian apocalyptic adventure.

This is to my mind a mistake. It is not the "Orthodox" answer. The arts must be given a high priority by the church because they represent evidence of the mind of our culture. Yet when we emerge in the public mind in connection with the arts, it is in reaction to one exhibit or another, one artist or another. Our reaction is that of outrage rather than engagement. In return, many artists react against us rather than with us. We are, after all, engaged in the task of discovering meaning. Nothing involves us, in common with the others among whom we live, more vividly than the arts. We must commission and sponsor artists among us not to create our own alternative version of the arts, but rather to contribute dialogically to the culture of which we are a part.

This is, I am convinced, the best way in which we can "de-familiarize" the meanings we assign to the stuff of our lives and see them again, anew, in the gospel. The "re-evangelization" of the postmodern world involves our own role in the larger dialogue. If the church confines itself to its own space, as many would have us do and even as some would have the Constitution make us do, to impart its wisdom and assign its meanings, that in essence deprives us of a role in shaping meaning at all. There is no longer any real dialogue. We become merely the assembly of believers for mutual reassurance.

So I have offered only some perspectives from the East European experience, with some possibilities offered to the world to which I belong. I do not find an enthusiastic response among my colleagues in the West, except of course among their artists. Among theologians, at least, the arts are an adjunct at best, in parallel to their essentially decorative function in most of our churches.

Nor, despite its resources, can I offer our own tradition in the U.S. as a model. We are replete with converts, especially in the realm of the clergy, whose proportion far outnumbers those in the pews. We are from a tradition in which the arts have been not only the vehicle for meaning, but also, in our iconographers and great master interpreters in literature, the source of theological awareness. Yet the search for Orthodoxy has been deployed so often in Western terms that we Orthodox often emerge in our apologia very frequently as not an open, dialogic assembly, but as the very reassurance of a stolid, enduring, even chiseled Meaning.

The forms we Orthodox could engage, using our very hospitality to the visual and musical and literary arts, have been borrowed wholesale from other times and other places: Byzantine music, Russian iconography, Galician chant, Ukrainian embroidery — all promulgated not only by our own ethnics, but often most insistently by Irish and Anglo-Saxon converts. The cultural segmentation of the church becomes even more segmented, within discrete eras and ethnicities. In our tradition in the U.S. we do not "de-familiarize" and challenge categories of meaning. Instead, we "re-familiarize" our people with cultural models from other times and places.

Our models, however, for both the West and the East can be found in a real look at the greatest moments of our much discredited missionizing. If we explore the past relationship our Puritan forebears had with the Indians when they came to these shores, we find that the history is not the uninterrupted cycle of forced missions and destruction of native forms that are part of the stereotype. That is, in fact, the "second wave" of early American scholarship, the one that sees the Puritans as sour-minded slaughterers. Indeed, the recent scholarship by young innovative scholars like David Thomson regarding Native American missions holds some surprises. Among Algonquins in the Massachusetts Bay colony the most vital Indian missions (and alas the most fully betrayed) were those communities in which the native Christians were true to their own cultural forms and modes of organization. John Eliot and Roger Williams respected those forms, lent an autonomy to native American villages, and looked at times upon the gospel's emergence in a Native American environment with awe and with a degree of "de-familiarization" of their own.

Russian missionaries in Alaska engaged in a similar process. Detailed dialogue with interested native shamans was an initial part of the dialogic exchange. That followed with a translation of the gospel and liturgical texts into native Alaskan languages, with a due respect for the cultural translation of the visual arts important in our iconography into forms compatible with native traditions. Bishop Inokentii Veniaminov acted as anthropologist as well as linguist in his translation of the terms of the gospel into new, "de-familiarized" but recognizable forms of their shaman antecedents. *Angu-rum Angali,* the "light and the day of God" as an equivalent of the "Kingdom of Heaven" in the gospel, or *qanhunyaq,* "existing Thrice simultaneously," was chosen by the bishop after long exchanges with shamans, creoles, and a study of native stories and myths. Native Aleut, Yupik, and Tlingit stories and forms were studied for their own sake as well, for the "de-familiarization" they could offer to the deadened terms of our own way of perceiving the gospel. Veniaminov's conviction was that Christianity was immanent in a culture already existing, that the beauty of the gospel form could be translated into the beauty and garb of the culture into which it was to be made manifest. Hence evangelization was not an imposition of a truth, but rather a recognition and development of that icon already existing.

Our tendency as Christians is, like that of the early Puritans opposed to Eliot's evangelizing, to see postmodern thought and culture as alien territory occupied by depraved tribes. Yet if Yurkevich and Veniaminov and Florensky and Bakhtin offer any insights, it is that all peoples contain the interpretative grist to allow the gospel to "affect the heart" of our understanding. Postmodern culture rejects God in much the same way that William Blake the mystic poet rejected Nobodaddy, "Nobody's Daddy," the empyrean God in which the authorities believed, but who hurled his excrement upon the masses beneath.

Postmoderns are much like the Soviets, many of whom eventually felt themselves drawn to the faith not by their rational understanding, but by their appetite for completion. Those who found illumination in the gospel did not "find themselves," in the modern idiom. They discovered who they had always been. Postmodern culture is a culture that has already received fossilized forms of the gospel once vital perhaps in another place and time, but already rendered so familiar as to have lost significance. Those forms need not be "re-presented," but rather de-familiarized. And I believe that it is our arts, which invariably present at least the act of seeking, to which we must turn our attention.

The forms of our arts are accessible by their very nature; they are the products of the culture to which we belong. Although for historical reasons the West has emphasized the didactic elements, particularly in the religious arts, there are Christian artists among us who can participate in a deeper process of evangelization than recapitulating truths or repeating sentiments that already exist. In concrete terms, the arts need attention in our seminaries, where they are pathetically underrepresented, in academic forums like this one, where they are seldom present, and in endowments and institutes, where if they are recognized they are the first to be cut in a crisis. (The National Council of Churches occupies itself with issues of social justice; the position dealing with Arts and Liturgy was among the first to be cut at the first hint of budget constraint.) The arts have no prestige among us, but they deserve a position of privilege and honor, for they are our primary dialogic forum.

Finally, (and of course I must conclude with what is axiomatic for any Orthodox) worship is that environment where we can reclaim the fruits of that artistic engagement. For if all people engage in some form of dialogue with each other, only we believers engage in ritual dialogue with our God. It is in that environment that we are "reciprocally defined," and if in that environment we cannot evoke a sense of the holy and the sacred, and bring forth for us those meaning-bearing symbols that effect the Word, then we truly have nothing to offer. There is nothing, in effect, to convey in the act of evangelization. The heart as a seat of identity and understanding, of which intellection is only a part, is a very real category in our thought. The process of "de-familiarization" assures a continuing effort to convey the "strangeness" and perpetual "newness" of the gospel.

We must not read Augustine's famous passage "our hearts are restless until they rest in Thee" in such a way as to assume that this "rest" is a quiescent activity. Rather, this kind of rest is but the assurance of that very postmodern quest for "identity." And our nature as creatures of God is ever to struggle, ever to quest, ever to disturb each other and ourselves in the discovery of what can never ever be familiar. The completion of that Augustinian passage, which on its surface seems so antithetical to our age, is a passage that holds a like place of honor in the Christian East. Gregory Nazianzen asserted that always, even in the next life, we ever grow from "glory to glory." In worship, in dialogue, in the immanence of God not only in Creation but also in our processes of artistic representation and communication and co-being — yes, of believers and unbelievers together — we find that process of growth. His is the glory. Ours is the promise.

Truth Decay: Rethinking Evangelism in the New Century

TODD E. JOHNSON

Truth Decay? A Book and Its Cover

Although it is often true that you cannot judge a book by its cover, in the case of this essay I hope the title is fairly representative of what it contains. For example, the subtitle "Rethinking Evangelism in the New Century" implies that there is more than one way to evangelize. Accordingly, I will be suggesting that it is time to consider new — or at least different — methods of evangelization than are found in many of our churches. Similarly, the title "Truth Decay" implies that current forms of evangelization are compromising the "truth" of the Christian message.

This term "truth" can be a slippery one, however. It is helpful to remember that this presentation is made at a conference that is examining the proclamation of the gospel in a postmodern world. Postmodernity, although resisting an easy definition, is a period of time when the idea of an objective "truth" is viewed with suspicion. Postmodernity is not a single philosophical movement, but rather a cluster of movements that range from the skeptical — those who would maintain that truth is completely subjective and without normativity — to the affirmative — those who would retain the concept of truth but also assert that truth is relative to a particular community and its worldview.[1]

1. For a helpful introduction to postmodernity in its various forms see Pauline Ma-

118

Christians who subscribe to the former would fit the label of what Robert Bellah called "Sheilaism." Sheilaism is the practice of a do-it-yourself spirituality, in which you mix and match your spiritual traditions, customizing religious practices to fit your understandings of "god, faith and truth."[2] Skeptical postmodern Christianity in a consumer culture has resulted in the growth of service-oriented churches as well as the preponderance of "spiritual but not religious" Christians.[3]

Christians who subscribe to the latter would emphasize the interpretation of the Christian tradition by subgroups within that tradition. My own work would fit into this category. One of the models I have suggested for church ministry is that of three concentric circles. The largest of these circles is the Christian tradition defined by the norms of a triune God revealed foremost through the Paschal Mystery. The second circle is the interpretation of the Christian tradition by denominations or theological traditions. The innermost circle is the application of the second level of interpretation by the local congregation to its unique communal life and worship. Affirmative postmodern Christians would place a priority on the innermost circle, where the abstract beliefs of the outer two circles are enacted in concrete pastoral acts.[4] Primary truth for the community is contextual rather than abstract, local rather than universal.

The focus of this essay is to further explore the implications of this three-tiered model in terms of evangelism. This analysis will for the most part exclude the assumptions of skeptical postmodernism. Instead it will focus on "truth" as agreed upon by the local community. The thesis of this essay is that in becoming a disciple — or in assimilating the truth of the local community — one must be socialized or enculturated into the community, learning its language, internalizing its values, and participating in its meaning-making activities such

---

rie Rosenau, *Post-Modernism and the Social Sciences: Insights, Inroads, and Intrusions* (Princeton: Princeton University Press, 1992), pp. 3-24.

2. Robert Bellah et al., *Habits of the Heart* (New York: Perennial Library, 1986), pp. 220ff.

3. For a detailed examination of this phenomenon see Richard Cimino and Don Lattin, *Shopping for Faith: American Religion in the New Millennium* (San Francisco: Jossey-Bass, 1998).

4. Todd E. Johnson, "Practical Guidelines for Worship in Social Ministry," in *The Ministries of Worship*, The Complete Library of Christian Worship, vol. 7, ed. Robert Webber (Nashville: Star Song Publishing, 1994), pp. 486-88.

as liturgies and ministries. Evangelism is the first step in this process of enculturation into the Christian church, not in general but as interpreted and implemented by the local community. My underlying assumption is that when evangelism fails to be congruent with catechesis, liturgy, and ministry, the truth of the local community is compromised.

The Canon of Protestant Evangelism

When one hears the term "evangelism," various images may come to mind. You may envision someone passing out tracts on the street corner. Maybe you imagine a faithful church member persuading a new neighbor to come to his or her church; or possibly you have a less traditional understanding of evangelism and think of caring for the homeless, persons with AIDS, and so on. Sooner or later I would guess that the picture of an evangelistic preacher in front of a great crowd (or at least in front of a television camera) would cross your mind. In some ways this is the most obvious expression of evangelism in North America, and has certainly been the most influential.

The roots of this revivalistic model of evangelism can be traced to the practice of Scottish Presbyterians gathering for "sacramental seasons" in the seventeenth century. Sacramental seasons were gatherings of clans in the highlands where a Presbyterian minister would lead the people in a few days of Bible teaching, prayer, and hymn singing — all leading to self-evaluation and repentance, and concluding with the Lord's Supper. Sacramental seasons were times of reaffirming one's baptismal faith. These were not considered to be one's regular diet of worship, but provided sacramental worship for those who did not have regular access to clergy or a steady diet of preaching services. They also served as important social functions as they allowed for interaction between various clans living in semi-isolation.

This supplemental form of Christian ritual came to North America with the Presbyterians. This pattern of Christian gathering was soon assimilated by numerous Protestant groups, particularly the Methodists, but also Episcopalians and even Quakers. This became the cornerstone for the "Camp Meeting" and the "Tent Revival."

However, here in North America there was a different religious context than in Scotland. One could no longer assume the participants in these meetings were baptized, or if they were baptized, that they were "regenerate." This led to the inclusion of an "altar call" before the celebration of the Lord's Supper in these meetings. The ritual pattern of these meetings was threefold: the preliminaries (i.e., singing, testimonies, prayers), preaching, and response. Originally the primary response was the baptized renewing their faith and worthiness to receive the Lord's Supper. Over time it became an opportunity for those outside the faith to be convicted of their sin and receive the gospel message in a conversion experience. In both cases, the focus of these evangelistic rituals was the repentance of individuals, calling them into right relationship with God through Christ. This ritual pattern is called "frontier worship" and has had an impact on every Christian church in North America.[5]

This revivalistic liturgical form has taken many different expressions. One example is the Campbellite tradition manifest in the Disciples of Christ, who have weekly Eucharist yet practice believer baptism. Here the focus of the worship service is the calling of the faithful to affirm their baptismal vows in the celebration of the Table. Another form would be a typical Baptist liturgical pattern in which every worship service ends with an invitation to accept Christ into one's life, or recommit one's life to Christ. The response in this service is baptism (or occasionally re-baptism), often on the spot. Regardless, the understanding of the dynamics of the ritual is that salvation in Christ was being proclaimed and the authority for this proclamation was the unquestionable truth of the Bible. Although the people gathered would certainly see this liturgical form as an appropriate expression of worship of the triune God, the speech was directed as much to women and men in need of conversion as it was praise offered to God.[6]

Charles Finney in his 1835 work *Lectures on Revivals of Religion* provides a snapshot of the growing sense of pragmatism among Protes-

---

5. This term was coined by James F. White, *Protestant Worship: Traditions in Transition* (Louisville: Westminster/John Knox Press, 1989), pp. 171-91. For a more detailed description of the history of this liturgical form see Leigh Eric Schmidt, *Holy Fairs: Scottish Communions and American Revivals in the Early Modern Period* (Princeton: Princeton University Press, 1989). See also Lester Ruth, *"A little heaven below": Worship at Early Methodist Quarterly Meetings* (Nashville: Abingdon Press, 2000).

6. See Gordon Lathrop, "New Pentecost or Joseph's Britches? Reflections on the History and Meaning of the Worship Ordo in the Megachurches," *Worship* 72 (1998): 521-38.

tants in relation to evangelism and worship arising out of this frontier tradition. Liturgical historian James F. White succinctly describes this attitude as "[i]f something produces results, i.e., converts, then keep it. If it fails, discard it. This allows for plenty of experimentation but unsuccessful ties are quickly eliminated. So pragmatism became the essential criterion in worship."[7]

In short order, this threefold pattern of evangelism, which originally was a supplement to the classic fourfold pattern of Gathering-Word-Table-Dismissal, had supplanted it as an alternative form of worship. So pervasive was this pattern of frontier worship that many converts in eighteenth-century America were never exposed to more traditional forms of worship. For many Protestant Christians, the ritual pattern of preliminaries, preaching, and response along with the accompanying hymnody, testimonials, and firebrand preaching was consistent across both the evangelistic revival and the Sunday morning worship. There was an obvious connection between evangelism and worship in the frontier tradition. This would change in the twentieth century with the advent of youth ministry.

The Genesis of Youth Culture
and the Evolution of Youth Ministry

The concept of an extended period of transition between childhood and adulthood is a modern idea. In 1875 the Supreme Court ruled that tax money could be used for public high school education. Before this point only one in fifty attended high school. Now a growing population of adolescents remained at home and in school instead of entering the workforce. In fact the term "adolescent" did not come into prominence until Stanley Hall's two-volume work of that name appeared in 1905.[8] By the 1950s, adolescence not only was a social reality, it was a social movement. An entire youth culture was forming for the first time.

The roots of youth ministry can be traced back to the early-nineteenth-century response to the growing industrialization and sec-

7. James F. White, "The Americanization of Christian Worship or New Lebanon to Nashville," Unpublished Paper, 1995, p. 6.

8. David Bakan, "Adolescence in America: From Idea to Social Fact," *Studies in Adolescence*, ed. Robert Grinder (New York: Macmillan, 1975), pp. 3-14.

ularization of England and the United States. Precursors of youth ministry are the Sunday School movement and the YMCA. The initial focus of youth ministry was in reinforcing the transmission of values from one generation to the next in the face of growing cultural resistance to religion. As "adolescence" came to mean more time away from family, it later became a central agent for this transmission.[9]

The methods used for youth ministry immediately after the Second World War focused primarily on large weekly youth rallies, often on Saturday night. In the era following ten years of depression and six years of war, youth ministry provided the opportunity for celebrative public gatherings and painted the picture of a brighter tomorrow through personal faith. Although these rallies existed into the 1960s, their effectiveness had long since passed as the times had changed drastically.[10] These rallies also coincided with the growing urbanization of the United States. It was in the cities where thousands of teenagers would gather at revivals to hear youth speakers such as Billy Graham.[11] This model of youth evangelism followed the typical pattern of frontier worship: preliminaries, preaching, and response, making it compatible with any number of churches worshiping in this pattern.

The effectiveness of these rallies varied depending on the audience and their predominant view of scriptural authority. The Bible was assumed to be authoritative by the evangelists at these rallies. To say that something was in the Bible was to appeal to the highest authority possible. But for a growing number of people, this authority had been seriously questioned in the Scopes Monkey Trial. Here the authority of the Bible was publicly challenged and defeated in the eyes of many Americans. High school education, which by the 1920s had become the norm for teens, increasingly emphasized "secular" values. No longer were Protestant Christian values seen as entirely compatible with a liberal arts education. The erosion of authoritarian presentations of the Bible had begun.[12]

9. Mark Senter, "The Youth for Christ Movement as an Educational Agency and Its Impact upon Protestant Churches: 1931-1979," Ph.D. diss., Loyola University of Chicago, 1989, p. 53.

10. Senter, "The Youth for Christ Movement," p. 42.

11. Senter, "The Youth for Christ Movement," p. 56.

12. For a formidable study of this trial and its lasting cultural and religious impact on American society, see Edward Larson, *Summer for the Gods: The Scopes Trial and America's Continuing Debate over Science and Religion* (New York: Basic Books, 1997).

In light of lessened certainty of biblical authority, new models of youth ministry sprouted in the 1940s and flowered in the 1950s. It is in this context that one should see the development of Youth for Christ and particularly Young Life and their relational approach to ministry. Young Life had its origins in 1940 in the vision of Texan Jim Rayburn, who initiated a transition from the rally model of youth ministry to the group meeting model. At these group meetings the leader would not presume that the Bible had any authority for the students, but would try to gain the trust of the high school students by developing a relationship with them, establishing the "right to be heard." Rayburn's conversational approach to public speaking was a distinctive of Young Life's ministry. He was different from preachers of his day, neither shouting nor pounding the pulpit. Instead, he just talked.[13]

Judging from its Leaders' Manuals of 1941 and 1970, Young Life's model of its weekly meeting changed little during this time. From 1950 on, these weekly club meetings replaced Saturday-evening rallies as the focus of youth ministry. A weekly meeting opened with fast-paced songs, followed by skits and games, leading to slow songs. With a shift in mood accomplished, a message was presented. Though biblically based, it was more thematic and practical than biblical exposition. The meeting concluded with music and prayer. The goal was to make the students as relaxed as possible to "break down the barriers" and earn "the right to be heard."[14]

There was more to the Young Life model than simply weekly meetings. There were annual trips to camps that provided excellent recreational opportunities in attractive vacation settings. There were even occasional youth rallies and other large-group meetings, all of which had the goal of conversion. But the most common supplement to the weekly meeting was the Campaigners Program. The Leaders' Manual defines Campaigners in the following way: "The club work is primarily outreach, introducing young people to the Person of Jesus Christ, while the Campaigners ministry is designed to continue in the Christian life in a vital growth process."[15] Though the goal of Young Life was to engraft the Campaigner into the local church, "the effec-

---

13. Senter, "The Youth for Christ Movement," p. 127.
14. Senter, "The Youth for Christ Movement," p. 269.
15. Senter, "The Youth for Christ Movement," p. 273.

tiveness of getting new believers into the local churches was unsatisfactory both to Young Life staff members and to [clergy]."[16]

The Young Life model and its correlative, "Incarnational/Relational Theology," were disseminated through professional youth ministry journals, books, and organizations, and quickly became the norm for parish and parachurch youth ministries in the 1970s.[17] It standardized a relational and conversational method of delivering a talk, in contrast to the authoritative biblical preaching of the youth rallies.

Further insight is gained into the methods of youth ministry when it is compared to the youth culture explosion of the 1950s. Through the postwar baby boom there developed a growing population that had access to both time and money, making teenagers a target market for the first time. Music, movies, magazines, books, and products of all sorts were created exclusively for adolescents. As one might imagine, teenagers became the recipients of a significant amount of advertising energy. Youth ministries had to compete with Madison Avenue in promoting a "product" that would provide meaning for the rock 'n' roll generation.

James Twitchell, in his insightful history of the relationship of advertising and American culture, cites the religious roots of advertising in the late nineteenth century as the impetus that gave rise to the religious quality of advertising in our century. It was literally the sons and daughters of Protestant clergy who took the message that "you are sinful, God offers salvation, accept the offer and you will be saved" and transformed it into "you have ring around the collar, Wisk can get the ring out, use Wisk and be saved from your dilemma." Like the holy relics of Christendom, access to these powerful items could in some way stave off the powers that threaten you.[18]

In a burgeoning consumer culture, youth ministry was competing with many other "products" in an expanding market. The growing tendency was to try to reach youth with the same techniques used by Madison Avenue on the Pepsi Generation: a confluence of message with media in which the two became indistinguishable. In a consumer culture, Christianity became a product to be tested, sampled, and compared to all of the other options available in the culture. The ritu-

16. Senter, "The Youth for Christ Movement," p. 274.
17. Senter, "The Youth for Christ Movement," pp. 329ff.
18. James Twitchell, *AdcultUSA: The Triumph of Advertising in American Culture* (New York: Columbia University Press, 1996), pp. 31-33.

als of evangelism and catechesis provided an entire generation with a new language for God that was not being used in worship. Herein lay the difficulty in moving teenagers from youth ministry into the church. Youth ministry sold Jesus to adolescents because they would "get something out of it." Where would they now worship?

From Youth Ministry to the "Seeker Service"

According to Mark Senter, youth ministry historian, 1979 marked a shift in youth ministry outreach from parachurch ministries like Young Life to the parish, as more and more churches hired youth ministers. Much of this followed the model developed by youth ministers Dave Holmbo and Bill Hybels in Park Ridge, Illinois in 1972. This church offered weekly youth gatherings that included competitive games, group activities, polished musical and dramatic performances, and an "evangelistic or pre-evangelistic message." By 1975 the meeting had grown to 1000 students a week and was divided into two meetings. In this same year Bill Hybels left this church and transferred the concept to South Barrington, Illinois. This youth ministry was the beginning of Willow Creek Community Church, which became "perhaps the best-known and most widely imitated church youth group in the nation in the 1980s."[19]

Hybels began Willow Creek when he was 23 as a youth ministry to 150 high school students, at that time meeting in a theater. As Hybels began to envision what sort of church could be built around this youth ministry, he canvassed the surrounding area, targeting white males aged 25-50 who were not attending church. Hybels surveyed the area, identifying what kept people away from church and what would bring them back. Hybels then proceeded to give the people what they wanted, what he calls a "biblical worship" that uses various forms of entertainment to avoid boredom. Within a year it was a congregation of 1000; in three years it was 3000. Now, twenty-five years later, over 15,000 attend Willow Creek on any given weekend.[20]

Liturgical historian James F. White points to the origins of the

19. Mark Senter, *The Coming Revolution in Youth Ministry* (Wheaton, Ill.: Victor Books, 1992), pp. 23-24.

20. Michael Maudlin and Edward Gilbreath, "Selling Out the House of God?" *Christianity Today*, July 18, 1994, pp. 21-25.

Seeker Service movement (what he also calls the megachurch movement or high-tech worship) as being the work of the Church Growth
movement, whose dean is Donald McGavran. It was McGavran who
wrote, "Those interested in liturgy find that church growth may say
very little about their concerns."[21] Little did he know how much he
underestimated the liturgical implications of his evangelistic para-
digms.

Hybels's method of facilitating the growth of his church demonstrates both Finney's sense of pragmatism and McGavran's liturgical
indifference. This is not to say that his method is not without its serious liturgical consequences. Hybels followed the Young Life model of
two ministry tracks in establishing Willow Creek. On the one hand he
had Seeker Services. These were not worship services *per se*, but outreach gatherings akin to the Young Life group meetings. Interestingly,
Seeker Services were held on Sunday mornings and then additionally
on Saturday evenings when "seekers" were most likely to attend.

According to Willow Creek materials, "Seekers are those people
who are in the process of making a decision for Christ or examining
Christianity."[22] The goal is to move these people from a decision for
Christ into church membership and affiliation in a small-group Bible
study, and attendance at Willow Creek's worship services on Wednesday or Thursday night. This element parallels the Campaigners com-
ponent of the Young Life model.

The Seeker Service follows fairly closely the Young Life model of
ritual as well. It begins with upbeat contemporary music, includes
drama, and employs the latest high-tech equipment for multimedia
presentations. Slower music is used as a transition to the talk, which,
as in the Young Life model, has biblical themes but is ultimately practical in orientation. What such services offer are relevant "talks" that
blend scriptural themes with practical advice on self-improvement for
a harried middle class. The preaching walks a fine line between
preaching the gospel and simply dispensing pop psychology.[23]

In a thorough study of Willow Creek, Gregory Pritchard has ana-

21. Donald McGavran, *Understanding Church Growth*, 3rd ed. (Grand Rapids: Eerdmans, 1990), p. 8.
22. Lester Ruth, "The Use of Seeker Services," *Reformed Liturgy and Music* 30
(1996): 48.
23. Gustav Niebuhr, "Where Religion Gets a Big Dose of Shopping Mall Culture,"
New York Times, April 16, 1995, p. 14.

lyzed the messages preached by Hybels and others on staff. Although they claim to preach a tradeoff between the blessings of the faith and the cost of discipleship, the evidence shows a decided imbalance on the side of spiritual gain.[24] This non-threatening message continues to attract the seekers to Willow Creek.

The source of Willow Creek's life has not been abandoned, as Willow Creek's focus remains with youth. High School youth meetings and Sunday School are high tech and multimedia. Aware that youth culture is always in motion, Willow Creek has special youth worship services designed to attract the unchurched and appeal to their cultural sensibilities as much as their spiritual longings. Nationwide megachurches are reaching out to the young by mimicking some of the most seductive elements of pop culture. The focus on youth arises from the reality that adults often look for churches that meet the needs of their children. Once these people are inside the door, the church presents them with the Christian message. At Willow Creek more than 60 percent of its teenage worshipers joined independently of their families.[25]

Willow Creek is not only successful, it is a cottage industry, with numerous churches subscribing to its materials and attempting to replicate its success. Some of these churches, denominational and independent, are less careful in their distinction between the "seeker service" and worship. Megachurches without this distinction commonly offer a variety of services, from traditional worship to seeker services, not unlike the offerings at the nearby "Movies 10" in the shopping mall.[26] Like the local shopping mall, megachurches offer a cornucopia of consumer items to attract seekers, and numerous opportunities for involvement, most of them amenities. Alongside small-group Bible studies and counseling, they offer aerobics classes, health clubs, day care and preschools, bowling alleys, and bookstores that sell a variety of related books and recordings.[27] Once again, we

24. Gregory Pritchard, "The Strategy of Willow Creek Community Church: A Study in the Sociology of Religion," Ph.D. diss., Northwestern University, 1994, p. 755.

25. Trip Gabriel, "MTV-Inspired Images, but the Message for Children Is a Moral One," *New York Times*, April 16, 1995, p. 14.

26. For more detailed analysis see Lester Ruth, "Lex Agendi, Lex Orandi: Toward an Understanding of Seeker Services as a New Kind of Liturgy," *Worship* 70 (1996): 386-405.

27. Gustav Niebuhr, "Where Religion Gets a Big Dose of Shopping Mall Culture," p. 14.

see that the ritual pattern used in evangelism is reflected in the culture of the church and its worship in particular.

Making Sense of the Stories

What can be learned from the preceding description of evangelization in North America? It would appear that the ritual patterns learned through evangelism are formative, providing one with a language for faith. In the recent analysis of American Protestantism, *Vanishing Boundaries: The Religion of Mainline Protestant Baby Boomers,* one case study illustrating the perceived lack of relevance of mainline churches describes a person who explicitly contrasts her church with the personable and accessible ministry she experienced in Young Life, particularly its rituals.[28] Although not everyone would identify their youth ministry experience as being incompatible with Christian liturgy, statistics suggest that this is a common experience. It is estimated that over 75 percent of Protestants under 50 had their primary religious experience through youth ministry and the marketing language we have identified.[29]

E. Byron Anderson summarizes a growing body of material from theology, religious education, and anthropology, concluding that ritual is the primary way one learns faith, for in ritual one is most fully engaged in the religious message. Anderson asserts that "liturgical practice is intrinsically formational and transformational. It is a means by which we come to know ourselves as people of faith and to know the God whom we worship."[30] Supporting John Westerhoff's argument, Anderson asserts that rituals are the most important influence in shaping faith, character, and consciousness.[31] Succinctly put, it is through ritual that we learn how to be a Christian.

Ethnographic research by Keith Roberts reinforces Anderson's

28. Dean Hoge, Benton Johnson, and Donald Luidens, *Vanishing Boundaries: The Religion of Mainline Protestant Baby Boomers* (Louisville: Westminster/John Knox, 1994), p. 23.

29. The figure 75 percent is one that has been used consistently over the last two decades regarding the percentage of Protestants of all denominations having a primary faith experience through youth ministry. This figure may be conservative in light of recent studies. Cf. *Christian Camps, Conference and Retreat Centers: 1990 Survey Report* (Wheaton, Ill.: Christian Camping International, USA, 1990).

30. E. Byron Anderson, "Liturgical Catechesis," *Religious Education* 92 (1997): 350.

31. Anderson, "Liturgical Catechesis," p. 352.

conclusions: myths are set forth in ritual and those myths define a worldview and a faith for the participant. Ritual norms in a changing world contribute to the plausibility of the mythic system they signify. Roberts's research indicates that the very sequence of the ritual defines the myth. Similarly, the language used in ritual conveys the implied sense of immanence or transcendence of God defined in the myth. Ritual is a primary vehicle of transmitting the tenets of the faith and teaching the worshiper how to interact with God.[32]

The implications of these conclusions for evangelization are clear: since the 1950s a large segment of the population has been evangelized and catechized with rituals that presented a mythic system incompatible with the rituals and accompanying mythic system of traditional Christian worship. The development of the seeker service was inevitable; for those who had come to accept the interpretation of Christianity presented through youth ministries a vehicle for its ritual expression was necessary. Although there are obvious precursors to seeker service worship (e.g., Robert Schuller's Crystal Cathedral in Garden Grove, California), it was Bill Hybels who made the connection between evangelism, catechesis, and worship for the baby boomers.

Even those who have never been exposed to youth ministry find seeker services accessible because they use the "religious" language of our society — advertising. In a culture saturated by consumerism, no translation to the mythic language of the "seeker service" is necessary. It has already translated the gospel into the categories of self-improvement and entertainment, and explicitly creates a ritual setting that reflects the business and consumer world of middle-class suburbia.[33]

It is tempting to pass this phenomenon off as a recent discovery. However, the concept has been part of the Christian tradition for centuries, as reflected in the phrase "lex orandi/lex credendi" or "the law of belief is the law of prayer." This adage implies that we learn how to pray first and from this learn what to believe. Many liturgical theolo-

32. Keith Roberts, "Ritual and the Transmission of a Cultural Tradition: An Ethnographic Perspective," *Beyond Establishment: Protestant Identity in a Post-Christian Age,* ed. Jackson Carroll and Wade Clark Roof (Louisville: Westminster/John Knox Press, 1993), pp. 74-98.

33. See Paul Goldberger, "The Gospel of Church Architecture, Revised," *New York Times,* April 20, 1995, Section C, pp. 1-6; and Gustav Niebuhr, "Protestantism Shifts Toward a New Model of How 'Church' Is Done," *New York Times,* April 29, 1995, Section I, p. 12.

gians would argue from this phrase that Christian worship is primary theology and all other theology is secondary theology, or reflections on the worship of the community.[34]

Although at first blush this concept seems unnatural, it is actually very common. My wife and I have been graced with five children, the last three being triplet daughters. As you can imagine, there are moments when the children, particularly the triplets, have disagreements. When this occurs, I do not sit down and explain the virtues of reconciliation and confession and invite them to consider the importance of relationships in our family. No. What I say is, "Tell your sister you're sorry!" I teach the behavior first and trust they grow into the meaning of the behavior over time.

Isn't this the way we all learned our American history? After all, who of us born in America was taught the history of our country, our political and economic philosophies, and then at the appropriate age was asked if we would like to pledge allegiance to the flag? No, we all were taught to stand, place our hand over our heart, turn to the flag and pledge our allegiance to our country through this flag ritual. It is within the context of this ritual that we learned our country's history, our political and economic philosophies.

The bottom line is that we are socialized into our communities by behaviors as well as beliefs. The extent to which our processes of socialization complement and reinforce each other determines the "truth" of our Christian communities. Practically speaking, this requires that there must be an intentional congruence between the language and methods of evangelization, catechesis, worship, and ministry in our churches. If our youth ministry is not preparing our youth for the culture of the rest of the local church, our youth will often go elsewhere where the culture is more compatible with their youth ministry experience, or they will stay and try to negotiate the culture of the church, often resulting in multiple worship services.

---

34. For a helpful essay on the history and meaning of *lex orandi/lex credendi* see Avery Dulles, "The Reciprocity of Belief and Prayer," *Ex Auditu* 8 (1992): 85-94. For a survey of theologians who would maintain the primacy of liturgy in the theological task one would be well served by considering the works of Orthodox theologian Alexander Schmemann, *Introduction to Liturgical Theology* (Crestwood, N.Y.: St. Vladimir's Press, 1966); Roman Catholic Aidan Kavanagh, *On Liturgical Theology* (New York: Pueblo, 1984); Lutheran Gordon Lathrop, *Holy Things: A Liturgical Theology* (Minneapolis: Fortress Press, 1993); and Methodist Geoffrey Wainwright, *Doxology* (New York: Oxford University Press, 1980).

The frontier and seeker-sensitive traditions have mastered this by bringing worship, ministry, education, and evangelism into line with one another. Other traditions have co-opted elements from these traditions for evangelism, education, and youth ministry, but such elements do not necessarily fit their theological, ecclesial, or liturgical framework, and may create dissonance and competing theological models within the church. This can happen on the local level where a liturgical church hires a youth minister or minister of evangelism who is insensitive to or ignorant of the larger tradition being served. This is also happening on the denominational level as denominations seeing a decline in membership turn to seeker-sensitive models for new church plants — even though they are a poor fit with the denomination's tradition — because they are effective in attracting new members. What can be done to prevent this disconnection?

The Catechumenate: A Historical Model of Evangelism Reconsidered

The practice of evangelism as an intentional enculturation of people into the church's culture is not new. In fact, it was the practice of the Christian churches as early as the second century. It was this historical pattern that was the germ of the new rites of adult initiation introduced by the Vatican in 1972, for the first time differentiating between infant and adult baptism in the Roman Catholic tradition. The important distinction was that the adult rite was a process stretched over time, not a single event. This process involved four stages: Evangelization, Catechesis, Enlightenment, and Mystagogy. This ritual pattern is known as the Rite of Christian Initiation of Adults. The success of the RCIA is evident in the imitation by Protestant churches,[35] as well as the call from within the Catholic Church to rethink the practice of infant baptism.[36] "The RCIA is much more than a collection of rites and rubrics; it is ultimately a pastoral statement

---

35. For example, see Robert Webber, *Liturgical Evangelism* (Harrisburg, Pa.: Morehouse Press, 1992).

36. For two notable Catholic theologians who have called for a de-emphasis on infant baptism see Aidan Kavanagh, *The Shape of Baptism: The Rite of Christian Initiation* (New York: Pueblo, 1978); and Ray Noll, *Sacraments: A New Understanding for a New Generation* (Mystic, Conn.: Twenty-Third Publications, 1999).

that re-envisions both the mission and character of the Christian community."[37]

The promulgation of the RCIA also implies that there are "enough master Christians to apprentice catechumens in the intricate art of Gospel living."[38] The RCIA is based on the belief that the Christian faith is an organic process, a journey, not a juridical process of getting one's sacramental inoculations. The goal is to involve the RCIA candidate in an exercise of thoroughgoing transformation, for both the individual and the congregation. The emphasis on personal and corporate transformation makes the RCIA more akin to a twelve-step program than a typical Christian educational curriculum.

The RCIA is patterned after the many similar processes of initiation practiced by Christian churches in the third and fourth centuries. Although they differed from location to location, they had a structural similarity. They also had another similarity: the emphasis on learning the Christian lifestyle, which excluded many professions and cultural practices. For example, in Hippo the baptismal candidates were not permitted to bathe from Ash Wednesday to Holy Thursday. This was as much a practice of asceticism as it was a separation of the catechumen from the practice of attending the public baths.[39]

Franciscan Kenan Osborne, reflecting on the progress of the past century, has noted that there was as much if not more philosophical shifting that occurred as there was social or technological change. Using the vocabulary of Foucault, Osborne states that the epistemé (or overarching worldview) that has served Christian theology for the past century has faded if not disappeared. His conclusion is pointed: "To continue to filter one's theology through a dying epistemé is meaningless."[40] From this perspective a new Christian worldview must be appropriated to make evangelization possible.

Some theologians have suggested that the patristic era is exactly the period the churches should turn to for guidance in responding to the postmodern world. These scholars maintain that the pluralism of postmodernity is best reflected in the history of Christianity in the

37. William Harmless, *Augustine and the Catechumenate* (Collegeville, Minn.: Liturgical Press, 1995), p. 9.

38. Harmless, *Augustine and the Catechumenate*, p. 9.

39. Harmless, *Augustine and the Catechumenate*, p. 251.

40. Kenan B. Osborne, *Christian Sacraments in a Postmodern World: A Theology for the Third Millennium* (Mahwah, N.J.: Paulist Press, 1999), p. 57.

sub-apostolic, pre-Constantinian church, sometimes referred to as "classical Christianity."[41] One such scholar, Robert Webber, suggests that the ancient paradigm of faith was one marked by mystery, symbol, and community. As the Christian tradition moved through time, it became more institutional in the medieval period, and more text-centered in the Reformation. In the Enlightenment that ushered in modernity, Christianity became increasingly individual and analytical. Webber claims that the postmodern world is reacting not only to the certainty of truth offered by modernity, but to the institutional and textual emphasis of the medieval and Reformation periods. Therefore, according to Webber, the church's best plan of survival is to return to the ancient triad of mystery, symbol, and community to communicate the gospel to a postmodern world.[42]

Though very different from today in many ways, this period of "classical Christianity" was similar to our contemporary context of plurality. Yet within this classical period, where should we turn to learn from both the forms and themes of early Christian evangelization? I suggest we consider St. Augustine. Augustine is a good source for thinking about evangelization, for we not only have a clear picture of his evangelization, but also his treatise on evangelization, "On Catechizing Inquirers," written at the request of a deacon from Carthage.[43] Though Augustine was a catechumen since birth, he had never taken the Christian faith seriously.[44] Augustine was a seeker: his spiritual pilgrimage took him through both Manichaeism and neo-Platonism before finding the Christian faith. And his interpretation of the Christian faith reflects themes acquired along his spiritual journey, a life story that has many postmodern overtones.

Augustine's journey into the catechumenate began with his prestigious appointment as Milan's teacher of rhetoric. While here he encountered Bishop Ambrose. Augustine was attracted to Ambrose first

41. Robert Webber, *Ancient-Future Faith* (Grand Rapids: Baker, 1999), pp. 25-28. My concern is that Webber consistently refers to the early church tradition, not traditions, which would be both more accurate and more applicable to a postmodern Christianity.

42. Webber, *Ancient-Future Faith*, pp. 34-35.

43. Harmless, *Augustine and the Catechumenate*, p. 29. It should be noted that another one of the reasons for choosing Augustine is the comprehensive work of William Harmless on Augustine and evangelism, which makes this material readily available for an English-speaking audience.

44. St. Augustine, *Confessiones* 1.11.

by the quality of his speech — as well as the praise of his mother, Monica. His mastery of the rhetorical arts impressed Augustine, who himself was a master rhetorician. Of particular interest was Ambrose's use of allegory, which brought the biblical text to life, making even the most difficult text relevant, logical, and enticing. Augustine was likewise struck by the clever way Ambrose would lampoon the Milanese aristocracy, contrasting their penchant for fine garments and celebratory excess to the tempered Christian spirit of restraint.[45]

When Augustine petitioned for baptism, he was viewed suspiciously by Ambrose, who thought he was simply seeking a Christian wife. Augustine was accepted after meeting with Ambrose and having his intentions examined. Augustine joined the other "competentes" in the Lenten discipline of attending daily prayer twice a day. Here Ambrose used Scripture to reinforce the moral character expected of a Christian. It was not until the Sunday before Easter that Augustine and the other catechumens would hear their one and only sermon on the "Symbol of Faith" — the Creed. They were now expected to have the Creed explained to them, and memorized within the week for their baptism.

Baptism marked the first time Augustine would have seen the Christian mysteries or sacraments, for in the Eucharistic liturgy the catechumens were dismissed after the sermon. Once exposed to the sacraments the catechumens would hear a series of sermons explaining their meaning in mystagogical catechesis. What is important from this practice is the theme of ongoing education and formation of the baptized, as well as the practice of learning by doing followed by explanation.

Augustine transferred his experience of initiation to Hippo when he became bishop there. Augustine's pastoral insights reflect a discerning local church culture, a practice of retaining what was relevant and abandoning that which was not. For example, in Milan the theme of humility in discipleship was central, and embodied in the rite of footwashing as part of the process of initiation. But the rite was not imported to North Africa by Augustine because it was not as central a theme in his church's culture.

In Hippo, to initiate the process of enrolling in the catechumenate, a baptized member of the community would bring an unbaptized

---

45. Harmless, *Augustine and the Catechumenate*, pp. 82-89, 94-95.

inquirer to the bishop for examination. Two examinations followed: first, the baptized member would be examined on how well he or she knew this person and the reason for desiring baptism. This provided the context of the second examination, that of the inquirer. The potential candidate would be questioned about his or her motivation, often with dreams or visions accepted as evidence of a divine call.[46]

When the inquirer met with Augustine, he or she would be given a succinct overview of the Christian faith. If the inquirer assented to this presentation of the faith, he or she would be accepted into the catechumenate.[47] This began a one- to three-year period of formation leading to baptism. The catechumens would not attend unique services during this period. Instead, they would attend the regular daily and Sunday liturgies of the church; they were required to attend, possibly required to stand in a particular place, and they were expected to be attentive. Occasionally Augustine would stop and directly address the catechumens, making pointed applications of the topic at hand to their young faith.

Augustine's sermons introduced the story of salvation history, but the focus would be on the themes of the character of God's people, emphasizing morality and ethics. Augustine identified three types of catechumens: the well educated, the moderately educated, and those with little or no education. Augustine intentionally prepared his sermons to speak to each of these groups. It is clear that Augustine was thorough in his preparation, clearly identifying whom he was communicating with, what he was communicating, and how he was communicating it.[48]

When Augustine determined that the catechumen was ready for baptism, the catechumen would be enrolled as a baptismal candidate the first Sunday in Lent. This began a kind of "bootcamp" experience: no bathing, no sexual relations for the married, requirements of visiting the sick, distributing alms to the poor, and frequent all-night prayer vigils. At some point in Lent the catechumens would experience the scrutinies — a public denunciation of one's sinful inheritance — and would receive one of many Lenten exorcisms.[49]

Two weeks before Easter the catechumens would receive the

46. Harmless, *Augustine and the Catechumenate*, pp. 113-16.
47. Harmless, *Augustine and the Catechumenate*, pp. 118-20.
48. Harmless, *Augustine and the Catechumenate*, pp. 123ff.
49. Harmless, *Augustine and the Catechumenate*, pp. 244-99.

Creed, one week before receiving the Our Father. As was the case for Augustine in Milan, and in most churches at this time, it would not be until after they received the sacraments of bath, anointing, and Table, that these would be explained to them. A century earlier Tertullian warned against disappointment for those preparing to be baptized. At that time the rites of initiation into other religions involved an intricate apparatus to create the illusion of miracles occurring when one was initiated. Tertullian told those about to be baptized that their baptisms would not be sensational in the usual sense, but would be eternal in its consequences.[50]

Augustine's message and its delivery gripped his audience. When Augustine preached, "silence was rare; instead, the atmosphere was rowdy, emotionally charged, more like that of a sports arena than a modern church. It offered entertainment as well as instruction, theatrics as well as worship: its drama was salvation history; its script was the Scriptures; and its actors included everyone."[51] The invitation to consider the Christian faith was exciting but also substantive, not just sensational.

Augustine's catechesis was persuasive and engaging; it was liturgical — rooted in the ritual of the church. It was also transformational — focusing on the behaviors and attitudes required for life in this community. Although it provided knowledge, it transformed the person with more than knowledge alone. Instead it focused on training the head, heart, and hands, creating a new person through an intentional process of enculturation into an intentional community.

Truth Decay: Book and Cover Revisited

I began this essay by unpacking the title and its possible implications. I suggested that I would show that there is more than one paradigm for evangelization, and I offered three: Frontier, Seeker Sensitive, and the Catechumenate. I also suggested that some forms created dissonance for the church's proclamation of the gospel in ministry, education, and worship — not that they were bad in and of themselves, but they provided an inappropriate fit for some local communities. The

50. Harmless, *Augustine and the Catechumenate*, pp. 48-49.
51. Harmless, *Augustine and the Catechumenate*, p. 235.

context for this conversation is the postmodern paradigm, and the emphasis is on the local congregation as the locus for evaluation.

Having come to this point I would like to offer the following observations about evangelism in the postmodern world. First, evangelism will enculturate, but may not socialize, individuals into the local church. Phrased more directly, evangelism will give people a language for God whether or not it is intended to do so. This language may or may not fit the language used by the rest of the community.

Second, pragmatism was not the test for evangelism in the New Testament or the history of the church until the revivals of the Great Awakenings. Instead the test has traditionally been, and I would argue should remain, whether evangelistic practice provides a solid foundation for the making of disciples.

Third, seeker-sensitive churches are increasingly successful in socializing people into their communities by maintaining an intentional continuity and congruence between evangelism, catechesis, worship, and ministry. The question remains how successful they are in making disciples who follow the biblical mandate of picking up one's cross and following Christ. The conflation of consumerism and Christianity is at best a dubious achievement.

Fourth, evangelization must take into consideration the task of enculturating those children growing up in the community in ways that are consistent with the process of evangelization used for those outside the church. For those using the catechetical model this is particularly a problem. I have suggested elsewhere that if one is to be consistent, infant initiation should be a process, not a moment in time, and it will require a rethinking of the theology of infant baptism and its execution.[52]

Fifth, each church must ask itself the difficult question of how high it will raise the bar in terms of requirements for membership. Is the church willing to sacrifice potential numerical growth for the sake of theological continuity and integrity? What is it that makes each particular local church unique from its surrounding culture as a community transformed by the gracious love of the triune God through the paschal mystery? This may be the most dangerous question my re-

---

52. See my "Rethinking Infant Initiation," Catholic *Issues* online at http://www.adelphi.edu/ci/ISSUES/JOHNSON.HTM. See also Mark Searle, ed., *Alternative Futures for Worship*, Volume 2, *Baptism and Confirmation* (Collegeville, Minn.: Liturgical Press, 1987).

search raises, and is the elephant in the room for many churches and denominations today.

I have not meant this essay as a definitive statement on how to evangelize in the postmodern world. Instead, I hope to have identified the issues involved in maintaining the integrity of the Christian message while responding faithfully to the gospel mandate to make disciples. I am suggesting not a uniform program but an intentional and difficult discussion within our churches about our core values, how they are expressed, and where and how we draw boundaries between those within our communities and those without.

Orthodoxia, Orthopraxis, and Seekers

FRANK C. SENN

I am pastor of an "oldline" downtown Protestant congregation in a small city adjacent to a great metropolis. My congregation had two-thirds fewer members in 2000 than it had in 1950. That's the same percentage of baby boomers who have left their church of origin within this time period. My congregation also experiences today a stream of visitors to Sunday morning worship, most of whom can probably be regarded as unchurched "seekers." The mainline Protestant churches have devoted considerable energies to trying to increase the volume of that stream of seekers in order to reverse the membership hemorrhaging of the last two generations.

"Seeker services" became a practice in many mainline Protestant congregations during the 1990s. This phenomenon developed as a form of evangelistic outreach toward the large portion of the population in the so-called baby boom generation which is unchurched. It is part of the program of the so-called "Church Growth Movement" that originated in the studies of Donald McGavran, a Disciples of Christ missionary in India in the 1950s, who wanted to know why some missions grew and others didn't. His research resulted in a number of books that outlined principles for creating the conditions necessary for missionary success. In the early 1960s McGavran returned to the United States and became a member of the faculty of Fuller Theological Seminary. The principles of "church growth" that he developed were originally taught as missiological theory, but were applied to the North American cultural context in the 1970s. Aided and abetted by successful models in reaching the unchurched provided by such megachurches as the Garden Grove Community Church in Anaheim, California (the Crystal Cathedral) and later by the Willow Creek Community Church in Barrington, Illinois, "church growth" in theory and practice exploded beyond its earlier association with Fuller Seminary.

Ironically, McGavran initially thought that those interested in liturgy would find very little in "church growth" principles related to their concerns.[1] He proved to be a false prophet. "Church growth" has come to be almost exclusively concerned about worship — alternative worship, contemporary liturgies, and seeker services designed to attract and hold the unchurched. "Seekers" are defined as those adults who are searching for meaning in their lives. Among the baby boomers (those born between 1946 and 1964) are persons who have drifted away from organized religion, often as a result of some self-perceived negative experience with the church in their early years, but who, later in life, seek some kind of meaning that can only be provided by religion. Many of their "baby buster" children and "generation X" grandchildren grew up in homes that provided no religious formation or instruction, and they therefore had no previous formal relationship with a church. But they are evaluating Christianity or other religions on their own. Not having to overcome a previous negative experience, unchurched generation Xers especially tend to look for the "real thing," and often find it in Neo-Pentecostal fellowships like The Vineyard or Eastern Orthodox Churches, rather than in "seeker services" that are specially "marketed" to the suburban baby boomers. But market-oriented evangelism also aims to attract generation Xers by offering their own type of issues and music. Music is a major concern of the church growth gurus. It is one of their chief tenets that traditional church music is positively harmful to growing the church. Nothing shows the ideological, as opposed to the purely pragmatic, character of church growth more than the fact that its gurus continue to insist on this, in spite of the consistent rejection of the use of popular music by many of these younger adults and teens, as inappropriate for worship.

The "service" part of "seeker services" is hard to define. Perhaps the term survives because of its customary use in designating public worship in Protestant churches. But true "seeker services" are not de-

---

1. Donald McGavran, *Understanding Church Growth*, 3rd ed. (Grand Rapids: Eerdmans, 1990), p. 8.

signed to be acts of worship; they are acts of evangelism. "Seeker services" such as those developed by the Willow Creek Community Church do not employ distinctive Christian terminology or Christian symbols on the assumption that the unchurched are unlikely to understand or recognize them. Services are typically held in architectural settings in which the unchurched feel familiar and comfortable, such as theater-type auditoriums or gymnasiums. They use popular musical styles from the entertainment industry that supposedly connect with the musical tastes of most baby boomers. The music tends to be soloistic, and participation in the singing is not expected. The "message" (it is not called a sermon) is designed to show how basic Christianity applies to the practical issues of everyday life.

This is not worship as an act of devotion to God; nor is it even construed as worship. It is an article of faith among the proponents of "seeker services" that only believers can worship; seekers need to be evangelized. Rick Warren, pastor of the Saddleback Community Church in Orange County, California, writes in his popular how-to-do-it-like-us manual, *The Purpose-Driven Church*, "*Only believers can truly worship God*. The direction of worship is from believers to God. We magnify God's name in worship by expressing our love and commitment to him. Unbelievers simply cannot do this."[2] Below I will engage this assertion because I think it can be challenged. First, however, I want to discuss the spectrum of seeker-oriented services, explore their historical roots, and locate their larger cultural-religious context.

The Spectrum of Seeker-Oriented Worship

I need to discuss the spectrum of seeker-oriented worship in general because, in fact, few churches offer "seeker services" of the pure type. Churches like Willow Creek or Saddleback offer only "seeker services" on weekends; believer-oriented worship is held on Wednesday nights. But unless a congregation begins as a seeker-oriented mission, as Willow Creek and Saddleback did, it also has believers in its membership whose spiritual needs must be met. The usual solution is to provide a spectrum of services over the weekend, at least a traditional and an alter-

2. Rick Warren, *The Purpose-Driven Church: Growing Without Compromising Your Message and Mission* (Grand Rapids: Zondervan, 1995), p. 239.

native service, but sometimes with a range of options in between.[3] For example, the Community Church of Joy in suburban Phoenix, Arizona (an Evangelical Lutheran Church in America congregation) offers a spectrum of services that are categorized as "believer-oriented worship," "believer-oriented worship made visitor-friendly," and "visitor-oriented worship," which is Joy's version of a pure seeker service.[4] Those churches with fewer resources than these megachurches are advised by church growth workshops to offer "blended" services that incorporate contemporary elements within a traditional kind of service. Anecdotal evidence suggests that in congregations offering seeker-oriented, visitor-friendly, or "blended" worship, traditional liturgy does not fare very well even as one option within the spectrum of worship offerings.

Evangelical churches use these services with impunity. Churches with canonical regulation of liturgy, such as the Roman Catholic and Episcopal, do not offer such services as a "main attraction." Mainline congregations without canonical regulation of liturgy (or at least unenforced regulation), such as Lutheran (Missouri Synod as much as if not more so than ELCA), United Methodist, and Presbyterian, exercise their freedom to implement such services. In the case of the United Methodist and Presbyterian churches, their splendid new official worship books were authorized just at the point in time when seeker-oriented or contemporary worship was taking off, and these worthy books languish for lack of use. But the order of service typical of "seeker services" is also typical of the orders used in Methodist, Presbyterian, and other Protestant churches in North America before the advent of their new worship books.

The usual format of the "seeker service" is as invariable and ecumenical in its own right as the historic Western liturgy. In comparing the orders of service used in Calvary Memorial (Community) Church in Oak Park, Illinois, and Faith (Missouri-Synod) Lutheran Church in Troy, Michigan, whose worship folders I procured, I find an exact correspondence, as follows:

Pre-service music provided by the praise band
Welcome and announcement

3. See Lester Ruth, "Lex Agendi, Lex Orandi: Toward an Understanding of Seeker Services as a New Kind of Liturgy," *Worship* 70 (1996): 386-405.
4. Timothy Wright, *A Community of Joy: How to Create Contemporary Worship* (Nashville: Abingdon, 1994), pp. 56-57.

Opening medley of praise
Time of prayer
A celebration of a sacrament (Baptism or Holy Communion)
Offering
Message
Response
Blessing

Not only is this order of service a standard form of seeker-oriented or alternative worship, it has a history of use as the most typical form of worship in American Protestant churches. Its lineage can be traced to what James White calls "frontier worship."[5]

The American Revival Tradition and Seeker-Oriented Worship

The "church father" of the frontier tradition is Charles G. Finney, who was converted in the camp meetings that swept upstate New York in the 1820s. He became a Presbyterian minister, but when he found the Princeton theologians unsympathetic to revivalism with its Arminian theology he became a Congregationalist and served as pastor of the Broadway Tabernacle in New York City. Later he moved to Oberlin, Ohio, where he served as a pastor, as professor of theology, and finally as president of Oberlin College. His great accomplishment was to bring the "new measures" of the frontier camp meetings into the established churches, even in the cities. He did so with an utter disregard for traditional Reformed or Puritan liturgy. He states in his *Lectures on Revivals of Religion* (1835):

> The fact is, that God has established in no church, any particular *form*, or manner of worship, for promoting the interests of religion. The scriptures are entirely silent on these subjects, under the gospel dispensation, and the church is left to exercise her own discretion in relation to all such matters.[6]

5. James F. White, *Protestant Worship: Traditions in Transition* (Louisville: Westminster/John Knox Press, 1989), pp. 171ff.
6. Charles G. Finney, *Lectures on Revivals of Religion*, ed. William G. McLoughlin (Cambridge, Mass.: Harvard University Press, 1960), p. 251.

Finney's contribution to the development of Protestant worship in America was considerable. His only principle was pragmatism: do what it takes to save souls. Choirs and organs appeared in churches whose Reformed and Puritan ancestors had once banished them. Pulpits were whittled down in size to simple lecterns for holding a Bible and the preacher's notes; the preacher was given a stage on which to move about exhorting his listeners. The sacramental furniture — fonts and tables — were almost hidden from view; the preached word was everything. From their origins in the Scottish Presbyterian sacramental seasons, revival meetings became gatherings with no meal, eliciting decisions for Christ with no body and blood, issuing altar calls to no altars. The threefold ritual structure of (1) praise, prayer, and offering, (2) testimonies, Scripture, and sermon, and (3) response was ubiquitous. Substitute a praise band for the organ, a drama for the testimonials, and an invitation to Christianity 101 classes or small groups for the "anxious bench," and you have the service of Willow Creek Community Church and its numerous imitators. It's a format that comes right out of the evangelical revival tradition, now transplanted from frontier camp meetings to suburban corporate campuses.

The Crisis of Worship in the Enlightenment

The fact that this form of worship strikes people as "modern" is significant because in its general principles it is as modern as the Enlightenment. The revolution in worship that occurred in the Age of Enlightenment was a rejection of the motto to which J. S. Bach subscribed, that worship is rendered *soli Deo gloria* — "to the glory of God alone," in favor of the principle that everything done in worship must edify the congregation.

The Enlightenment provides the cultural cradle of seeker-oriented worship — as well as of the general approach to worship in all Western Christian traditions since the eighteenth century. The brochure advertising this Conference of the Center for Catholic and Evangelical Theology on "The Crisis of Christian Worship" says that "The Church has been undergoing a crisis of Christian worship ever since Vatican II." In fact, the crisis generated by the liturgical reform coming out of the Second Vatican Council and similar reforms in non-Roman

Catholic churches has been only the latest phase of a general crisis in worship (both Christian and Jewish) since the Enlightenment.

The profound change that occurred in the eighteenth century is that the focus of worship shifted from God to humanity. Once upon a time liturgical rites were simply taken for granted as a way to approach God and to celebrate God's gracious presence among and for human beings. One could argue that the concern of the Reformation as a liturgical movement was to eliminate a superstitious approach to rites and to offer a non-idolatrous worship to the true and living God. But this God and his gracious dealings with human beings through means of grace instituted by Christ was still the focus of worship. Forms of worship and liturgical practices that developed in the Reformation Era (Lutheran, Reformed, Anglican, and Roman Catholic) were solidified in the Age of Orthodoxy (or what I call the "Age of Certainty"[7]) so that theologically correct worship (*orthodoxia*) was offered to the true God. The concern was not so much the impact of liturgical orders and practices on the worshiper as the truth-value of those forms in the service of the true God. Liturgical ceremonies became badges of confessional identity. So Lutherans knelt for communion, the Reformed sat; Lutherans elevated the bread, the Reformed broke it; Protestants ate and drank the elements, Catholics enthroned the host in a tabernacle on the altar mensa and gazed at it in adoration during rites of Solemn Benediction and Corpus Christi processions. These practices were intended to reinforce the beliefs of the faithful by enacting doctrinal positions.

It was in the pietist reaction to the perceived sterility of orthodoxy, with its agenda of "converting the outward orthodox confession into a living theology of the heart," that the momentous change of emphasis began that would characterize worship in the Age of Reason, both in its rationalist and experientialist manifestations. The concern of rationalists was that worship should edify the congregation. Sermons were to address practical everyday concerns. The clutter of the baroque churches was cleared out and the walls were whitewashed so as not to distract worshipers from the word (which was sometimes inscribed on the walls in place of the images). In Lutheran music the syncopations of the old chorales were smoothed out, the

7. See Frank C. Senn, *Christian Liturgy — Catholic and Evangelical* (Minneapolis: Fortress Press, 1997), chapter 14.

complexities of J. S. Bach's contrapuntal church music were eschewed in favor of Handel's more homophonic choruses, and operatic arias replaced chant and recitatives since they could make more of an emotional impact on the hearers. In the Roman Catholic Church, the Synod of Pistoia in northern Italy in 1786 recommended that missals be published with vernacular translations and the Latin text in parallel columns so that the people could follow the mass, that the side altars be abolished, and that people receive communion at the mass rather than after. These efforts were squelched by Pope Pius VI in 1794, who smelled "Febronianism" in the synod's proposals. The ravages of the French Revolution on the Roman Catholic Church led to the Ultramontane reaction in the nineteenth century. Was the Enlightenment agenda for Catholic liturgical renewal suppressed or put on hold? Not quite.

Romanticism in liturgy has been seen as a reaction to Rationalism. To some extent it was, in that it valued the very liturgical orders and ceremonies that rationalism had discarded. But it valued the medieval ceremonies for the same reason that rationalism valued its simplified orders: as something that could move the human heart. Just as romanticism in general was a quest after an ideal age of the past by which to correct the perceived failings of the present age, so romanticism in liturgy was characterized by an attempt to retrieve historic forms that had been jettisoned by both the rationalists and revivalists. Thus there was a retrieval of ancient texts, of plainsong and Gregorian chant and Reformation chorales, of gothic architecture, high altars, candles, and historic vestments, incense, and silence. This not only recovered a sense of the majesty and mystery of God, or what Rudolf Otto called "the numinous," that is, the non-moral and non-rational element in religion, the *mysterium tremendum et fascinans;*[8] it also appealed to the romantic interest in aesthetics.

Even though romantic liturgists aimed to reconnect liturgy and church, in reaction to the individualism of the Enlightenment, the mysticism and symbolism of romanticized liturgy housed in its neo-gothic spaces also spoke to the personal yearnings of the romantic soul. It was more the idea of the church as the mystical body of Christ than the reality of the church as the historical people of God that in-

---

8. Rudolf Otto, *The Idea of the Holy*, trans. John W. Harvey (New York: Oxford University Press, 1958).

terested romanticism. The church's liturgy was objectified: it was something the church *had* rather than something that the church *did*.

The perceived "crisis" in worship brought about by the Second Vatican Council can be attributed to the fact that romanticism's concern for the beauty of holiness and for an adequate experience of the numinous got short shrift in the liturgical reforms. In those reforms a concern for intelligibility and simplicity to facilitate the "full, conscious and active participation" of the people called for in the Constitution on the Sacred Liturgy led to the simplification of rites, the elimination of textual duplications in the interest of streamlining liturgical orders, the use of indicative rather than subjunctive speech, and revolutionary changes in liturgical environment and music occasioned by vernacularization and inculturation. The same concerns were manifested, more or less, in the worship books of Anglican, Lutheran, Methodist, and Presbyterian churches.

The English Dominican Aidan Nichols has created quite a stir by his assertion that the modern liturgical movement shared the aims and methods of the Enlightenment, specifically its emphasis on intelligibility,[9] in its concern to make the liturgy more accessible to modern people. Perhaps what I am about to say will be more shocking yet, but I will say it: There is no difference in aim or method between the reforms of the historic liturgy enacted in the implementation of the Constitution on the Sacred Liturgy and the development of "seeker services." Both are concerned with making worship culturally accessible in terms of language, architectural settings, and ritual music. If modern megachurches don't look like churches, neither did the new buildings erected for worship in the wake of Vatican II. If "seeker services" make use of contemporary popular music, let's remember how we turned Simon and Garfunkel into church composers in the late 1960s as we imagined Christ as the "bridge over troubled waters." Both liturgical renewalists and church growth advocates have agreed that a modern liturgy requires contemporary forms of expression. Both liturgical renewalists and church growth advocates have recommended such expediencies of reaching out to our culture as planning worship that is congenial to certain segments within the congregation, or planning worship that represents a cross-section of the con-

---

9. Aidan Nichols, *Looking at the Liturgy: A Critical View of Its Contemporary Form* (San Francisco: Ignatius Press, 1996).

gregation, or traveling the multiple-service route. The hoped-for goal of such efforts is obviously to reach certain people. When Nathan Mitchell asserts that "the goal of ritual is not to produce a meaning, but to produce an *outcome* — *a person redefined by grace as God's own welcoming heart and hand*,"[10] he is saying something more than that rituals have transforming power (which they do); he is saying that rituals should accomplish conversion, which has also been the aim of pietists, rationalists, revivalists, and renewalists over the last two centuries. In the agendas of these movements, the purpose of worship was less to glorify God than to have an impact on the worshiper.

Nichols can be faulted for failing to recognize the modern liturgical movement's primary agenda of renewing the liturgy precisely as *leitourgia*, "the public work of the people," which does require the "full, conscious, active participation" of the people in a communal event. I also think that critics of current liturgical practice, such as Garry Wills in *Bare Ruined Choirs*, in lamenting the perceived absence of a sense of transcendence in contemporary worship, have missed the larger picture of the profound change in the attitude toward ritual that has taken place in the modern world, of which social historians and cultural anthropologists are now reminding us.[11] The reforms of Vatican II did not mandate the transvaluation of transcendence into intimacy, or an abandonment of elegant rhetoric, classical church music, and grand ceremonies for functional speech, popular music, and touchy-feely groupiness. These were our own cultural predilections. It needs to be pondered whether, on the one hand, modern Western society has a cultural capacity to express the *mysterium tremendum* or whether, on the other hand, the numinous — the essence of religion — isn't being rediscovered in the experience of community.[12] But we must also ask if a true sense of community is really what is being proffered to worshipers when worship is used to promote denominational causes and political ideologies, or to seekers when inoffensive creeds

---

10. Nathan Mitchell, "The Amen Corner," *Worship* 71 (1997): 71.

11. See John Bossy, *Christianity in the West, 1400-1700* (Oxford: Oxford University Press, 1985); Edward Muir, *Ritual in Early Modern Europe* (Cambridge: Cambridge University Press, 1997); Mary Douglas, *Natural Symbols: Explorations in Cosmology* (New York: Random House/Vintage Books, 1973).

12. See Lawrence A. Hoffman, *Beyond the Text: A Holistic Approach to Liturgy* (Bloomington and Indianapolis: Indiana University Press, 1987), pp. 149ff.

composed by pastors reflecting their personal spiritual journeys are paraded before the congregation.

Participation Is Public Affirmation

So pervasive is the notion that liturgical rites exist to make an impact on the worshiper rather than to provide true worship of the true God (who does desire worshipers, we're told in John 4:23), that rather than simply discount modernity's quest for meaningful ritual we should take the Enlightenment's humanistic concerns seriously and look at what anthropologist Roy Rappaport called "the obvious meanings of ritual."[13] In other words, we should ask just what it means that liturgical rites are done at all and what is accomplished by doing them.

The most obvious thing about performing liturgical rites is that the performance keeps the rites alive and, with them, the reality that the rituals communicate. To show how important this fundamental aspect of ritual is, consider that once upon a time public worship was offered to Zeus; but since Zeus lacks worshipers today his liturgical rites are no longer performed. Since Zeus's rites are no longer performed, the reality of Zeus is no longer publicly recognized. We may study the rites once performed in honor of Zeus; but they are dead rites. It takes the bodies and the breath of living human beings to give the rites life and the gods a voice. That's why the gods seek worshipers. If liturgical rites in honor of Zeus were once again performed, Zeus's reality would once again be accepted (at least by those who perform Zeus's rites).

This raises an interesting question about the relationship between practice and belief. We assume that someone might perform liturgical rites in honor of Zeus because one "believes" in him. Is this necessarily the case? Do the witches who perform the rites of wicca believe in witchcraft? Do Christians who invoke the Holy Trinity really believe in one God in three persons? We cannot jump to that conclusion, because belief is a private and inward state of being. It may be desirable that the performers believe in what the rites proclaim in or-

13. Roy Rappaport, "The Obvious Aspects of Ritual," in *Ecology, Meaning and Religion* (Richmond, Va.: North Atlantic Books, 1979).

der to avoid hypocrisy. But belief is not required for the performance of public and outward acts. What is required for the public performance of rituals is acceptance of the rituals — a willingness to do them and participate in them. Belief is a consequence of participating in the rites because it is the result of reflection on what has been encountered.

For most of us who do not originate great religions with their unique liturgical orders, our encounter with God comes through doing the liturgical rites — e.g., by reading or hearing the word and by administering or receiving the sacraments. So belief is not required as the first step in public worship; but performing the liturgical rite is the first step toward belief. As Rappaport suggests, "by performing a liturgical order the participants accept, and indicate to themselves and to others that they accept whatever is encoded in the canon of that order."[14] In other words, they publicly accept whatever reality that order celebrates, enacts, and confers. One has the option, of course, of not accepting what is encoded in the liturgical order; this is signified by not performing it. If enough people stop performing certain rites, those rituals will cease to exist as living realities and with them whatever reality the rituals communicated will also effectively cease. But if one does perform a ritual, one is bringing into being the reality it ritualizes by one's own body — by the words one speaks and the gestures one employs. This is true of both ritual leaders and ritual devotees, of both clergy and laity; both are performers who, by their participation, signal public acceptance of the liturgical order.

This public acceptance of the liturgical order does not require private belief. Certainly it is desirable that if I participate in a liturgy I should fully believe what it proclaims and celebrates. Christians certainly will want public acceptance and private belief to correlate, because Jesus taught that the Father desires worship to be done "in spirit and in truth." Yet I can also participate in liturgical rites while not fully or not always believing. Paul Tillich taught that belief necessarily includes an element of uncertainty and that there is no faith without doubt.[15] My private state of belief has no bearing on the pub-

---

14. Roy Rappaport, *Ritual and Religion in the Making of Humanity,* Cambridge Studies in Social and Cultural Anthropology 110 (Cambridge: Cambridge University Press, 1999), p. 119.

15. Paul Tillich, *The Dynamics of Faith* (New York: Harper and Row, 1957), pp. 16ff.

lic performance of the liturgical order. The only thing that has bearing
on it is that it is done.

People can attend a liturgy without believing in what it encodes. If
they are sincere in their unbelief they will not want to overtly participate in the liturgy so that it may be publicly seen that they do not accept it. The community may also not allow unbelievers to participate.
Hence, the unbaptized have not been welcome to share in the Lord's
Supper. They used to be ushered out (with a blessing) after the liturgy
of the catechumens, before the liturgy of the faithful began. But as
long as the church has hosted public worship, a mixed public of believers and unbelievers and those with states in between have been
welcome at least at the liturgy of the catechumens, and they were all
encouraged to participate by gradual stages in the true worship of the
true God. There was prayer that "seekers" would finally accept such
worship and the reality of the new creation in Christ that it encodes,
and that they would move toward belief, aided by the catechumenal
process. And precisely because ritual acts require bodily participation,
the very act of participating in the liturgical order indicates acceptance
of what is being proclaimed and celebrated, which itself may lead to
belief. That's why the catechumenal process puts more emphasis on
participation in liturgical rites and engagement in acts of ministry
than on indoctrination.

I said at the outset that I would challenge Pastor Rick Warren's assertion that unbelievers cannot truly worship God. I'm ready to do
that now. I would say that the public worship of God can be done by
believers or unbelievers, that public worship does not depend on an
inward disposition but rather on a public affirmation of the reality of
God by performing the liturgy. Participation in the liturgical order has
the possibility of moving the performer from the private state of disbelief to the state of belief, and therefore non-believing (or at least unchurched) seekers need to be engaged in true worship (*orthodoxia*) if
they are to move toward belief in the true God and respond to this
God in faith.

Nothing I have said here should surprise Lutherans. We teach and
confess that faith is not self-generated; it is a gift of the Holy Spirit
given when and where the Spirit chooses through the means of grace
— the preaching of the word and the administration of the sacraments. We got this notion from the Apostle Paul, who said in Romans
10 that "faith comes from what is heard." In order to "hear" the gos-

pel, it must be proclaimed. That requires preachers. The act of preaching raises the question of liturgical order, about which Paul had some pretty specific things to say. But the point I am making is that faith comes as a gift from participating in the prescribed ritual (an act of the body). Belief (an act of the head) is also formed as worshipers engage in the bodily act of participating in a ritual. The task of evangelism, therefore, must be to get seekers into such worship as a primary strategy of bringing them to belief. As Rabbi Lawrence A. Hoffman has also said, "Ritual is not the result of faith, but one of its causes that is why we need good rituals." In his view, ritual has the power to present an alternative worldview to the one that seekers currently inhabit, which is why he believes that "rituals work best if the script is seen as ancient and timeless."[16]

Since the Christian worldview is nothing less than the new creation in Christ, our evangelism experts have proposed exactly the wrong strategy. We should not be deconstructing the liturgical orders that celebrate and enact the new creation in order to accommodate the cultural expressions of the secular worldview; rather, through catechesis and ritual engagement we should be deconstructing the secular worldview within the seeker, who must "turn from idols to serve the living and true God" (1 Thess. 1:9). Liturgy that serves such a God cannot be faddish. As Aidan Kavanagh has said, "Liturgy either dies at the hands of the trendy, or it slays them. Neither alternative is comfortable, but the last is what Christian logos ultimately requires."[17]

Orthodox Christian Worship

If belief in the true God is to be formed, orthodox Christian worship must be performed. Churches are currently hung up on style rather than substance: what music to perform, what ambiance to create, what conveniences to provide. These are valid concerns. But the basic question must be: What God is being worshiped? I would say that it cannot be *presumed* that God the Holy Trinity is being worshiped in the

---

16. Lawrence A. Hoffman, *The Art of Public Prayer: Not for Clergy Only*, 2nd ed. (Woodstock, Vt.: Skylight Paths Publishing, 1999), pp. 119, 122.

17. Aidan Kavanagh, *Elements of Rite: A Handbook of Liturgical Style* (New York: Pueblo Publishing Company, 1982), p. 104.

liturgical orders used for alternative worship, for contemporary liturgies or seeker services. Those who plan such services may themselves believe in the Holy Trinity. But the private beliefs of the worship planners and leaders are irrelevant; what is relevant is what the liturgical order expresses. Unless the Name of the Father, the Son, and the Holy Spirit is invoked on the assembly in blessing and addressed as such in prayer, the liturgy of the Holy Trinity is not being performed and the reality of the Holy Trinity is not being publicly accepted.

Among many examples I could give, let me limit myself to two: the pervasive use of Jesus-songs in contemporary worship and the reduction of the Eucharist to the words of institution.

Jesus-songs are rooted in the evangelical pietist tradition that emerged in the seventeenth century. We know many of them well: "Jesus, Priceless Treasure," "Jesus, Thy Boundless Love to Me," "Ah, Holy Jesus." St. Bernard of Clairvaux in the twelfth century also wrote some tender love-lyrics to Jesus that were reprised in the seventeenth century by Paul Gerhardt and others. But these lyrics were not intended for use in the public liturgy; they were intended for household devotions. Yet even when they were incorporated into the liturgy, they were balanced by thoroughly trinitarian texts such as the *Gloria in excelsis* and the Nicene Creed or their chorale versifications. (The German Song-Mass [*Liedmesse*], based on the tradition of Luther's German Mass, is as trinitarian a liturgy as one can find; Luther's own hymns are thoroughly trinitarian, as befits their liturgical use, unless they are meditations on Scripture texts, such as "A Mighty Fortress Is Our God" and "From Heaven Above to Earth I Come.") Today, in the absence of such canticles and creeds in contemporary liturgies, evangelical worship becomes a unitarianism of the Second Person of the Godhead. Going through contemporary Christian music songbooks one finds a plethora of Jesus-and-me-songs such as "Shine, Jesus, Shine," "There Is a Redeemer," "Jesus, Lord to Me," "O Lord, You're Beautiful," and "I Have Decided to Follow Jesus." An overdose of these lyrics will undermine trinitarian worship.

This unitarianism of the Second Person continues at the Eucharist, which is no Eucharist at all when the Great Thanksgiving is omitted. Some liturgical orders, serving an efficient use of the parking lot, provide nothing more than the words of institution recited over bread and wine followed by the distribution, and sometimes not even a thank-you for the gift received before the dismissal. What is lacking when there is no eucharistic prayer? Nothing less than praise of the Father, the remembrance of the Son, and the invocation of the Holy Spirit, along with evocation of God's acts of creation, redemption, and sanctification, reactualization of the salvation event, petition for the benefits of communion, and anticipation of eschatological fulfillment in the banquet of God's kingdom. These themes are found, more or less, in classical eucharistic prayers, and there has been a conscious effort to include such motifs in new eucharistic prayers. The eucharistic prayer is the text, *par excellence,* that gives expression to the Christian worldview. Such texts make the worshiper sensitive to the world as God's creation, to discipleship as commitment to the servant-ministry of the Son, and to the new humanity manifested proleptically in the community of faith "called, gathered, enlightened, and sanctified" by the Holy Spirit.

The fact that I mention new texts means that I am not opposed to "recent acquisitions" to the tradition. But the purpose of developing new texts, music, and art is not to entice seekers by reducing the content of the faith; it is to give expression to the faith of the faithful as they find themselves thanking and praising, serving and obeying God in new historical circumstances and cultural settings. The widespread quest for spirituality today suggests that people may indeed be looking again for the numinous, the transcendent, and the eternal, especially a generation that has grown up largely without it. Unfortunately, they will not find it in liturgical orders that have been stripped of all God-content and that envision no way out of the dead end of the present age whose form is passing away.

The Trinity and Orthopraxis

Beyond content, trinitarian liturgy is expressed through a praxis that reflects the nature of the God who is a Community of Persons. As the late Edward J. Kilmartin, S.J., has written, "The mystery of the liturgy has a trinitarian structure in its execution and content."[18] The liturgy is the work of the church. But the church is the creation of the economic Trinity, which refers to God's decision to go out of himself in

---

18. Edward J. Kilmartin, S.J., *Christian Liturgy. I. Theology* (Kansas City, Mo.: Sheed and Ward, 1988), p. 102.

the acts of creation, redemption, and sanctification. The Son, sent by the Father to redeem a lost humanity by his sacrificial death, being raised from the dead and ascended into heaven, sends in turn the promised Holy Spirit from the Father to "call, gather, enlighten, and sanctify the whole Christian church on earth" and preserve it in such intimate union with Jesus Christ that it may be regarded as his body on earth.

The body of Christ that the Spirit enlivens reflects in its own life on earth the immanent Trinity, which refers to the inner life and inter-personal relationships of the Father, Son, and Holy Spirit. That is, trinitarian liturgy will be a communitarian act in which there is a division of roles within the assembly. Ignatius of Antioch, already at the beginning of the second century, saw an ontological relationship between the Godhead and the earthly assembly. Writing *To the Trallians*, he said:

> . . . everyone must show the deacons respect. They represent Jesus Christ, just as the bishop has the role of the Father, and the presbyters are like God's council and an apostolic band. You cannot have a church without these.[19]

If this scheme seems to allow no place for the Holy Spirit, it should be remembered that the baptized body of Christ is a Spirit-enlivened people. Christian baptism, the baptism authorized by Jesus to be performed "in the name of the Father and of the Son and of the Holy Spirit" (Matthew 28:19), is "by water and the Spirit" (John 3:5). The Holy Spirit is given to the baptized at their baptism. So the roles in the liturgical assembly are those of the father-bishop who presides, the Christic-deacons who assist, the apostolic-presbyters who preach and teach, and the Spirit-filled people who praise and pray.

It's not surprising that as various forms of unitarianism — of the Father or the Son or the Holy Spirit — became theologically dominant, the worship event came to be dominated by one role, whether the Reformed minister, the Catholic priest, or the charismatic leader. As Father Kilmartin puts it, trinitarian liturgy is a matter of structure as well as of content. It requires a differentiation of roles in the assembly. Reflecting the Holy Trinity in whose image the church has been

---

19. Ignatius of Antioch, Trallians 3:1; *Early Christian Fathers. The Library of Christian Classics*, I, trans. and ed. Cyril C. Richardson (Philadelphia: Westminster, 1953), p. 99.

created, these roles are distinct, not to be confused, and also inseparable. This includes not only the roles of the bishop, presbyter, and deacon, but also the role of the people whose "full, conscious, and active participation" (in the words of *The Constitution on the Sacred Liturgy*) is needed. Liturgy that lacks a role for the Spirit-filled people is not only non-trinitarian, it is non-liturgical; for *leitourgia* is "the work of the people."

What, Then, Do We Do with Seekers?

We invite them into the life of God which is the church, the body of Christ on earth. Like the first two disciples who found the Messiah, we invite others to "come and see" Jesus (John 1:46). While the liturgy is trinitarian in both content and structure, it is christological in substance. Christ is the *Agnus Dei* who takes away the sin of the world. Christ is the *Kyrios* seated at the right hand of the Father who receives our prayers and has mercy on us. Christ is the Son of God who emerges in the Gospels to fulfill prophecy (which should therefore be heard in the Old Testament readings) and to excite our hopes (as expressed in New Testament readings). Seekers should be invited to discover Christ himself in the church's age-old seeker service, the liturgy of the catechumens. As Andrew and Peter, Philip and Nathanael, and every one else come to see Jesus, the Holy Spirit enables them to glimpse the evidence that will allow faith to be born. They go from encounter to encounter with this man from Nazareth who always confounds their expectations.

In evangelization and catechesis seekers move from question to question: "Whom do you seek?" "Who is this man?" "But you, who do you say I am?" "What about you, do you want to go away too?" Despite Peter's confession and the predictions of Jesus' passion and resurrection, would-be disciples understand nothing until the Son of Man is raised from the dead and is confessed as "my Lord and my God" after the dark night of vigil. There wells up from the font a new creation brought forth by the life-giving Spirit who leads those who are now "enlightened" into the lighted hall for communion in the body and blood of Christ at the Lord's Table.

We will not easily set aside two centuries of fretting about what impact the liturgy is having on worshipers, and certainly the concern cannot be ignored — particularly in the way the liturgy is performed. But we may transpose that concern into the issue of whom worshipers are encountering in our liturgical orders. We may take comfort from the anthropological observation that if worshipers attend worship, they are publicly accepting what is transpiring in the liturgical orders, and that if they perform these rites regularly enough, they may be moved to belief in this God. We do not need to replace the divine liturgy with seeker services, but we can provide a catechumenate in which belief in the Holy Trinity is nurtured and honed into faith. This is not just theory; we ourselves may be living witnesses who demonstrate the hypothesis. Having experienced the depths from which the liturgy wells up, we are in a position to celebrate it in its fullness. The liturgy becomes ours only when we celebrate it. But having drunk from this well, we know what will satisfy others who ask for a drink. We know that its waters are life-giving and refreshing.[20]

20. See Jean Corbon, *The Wellspring of Worship*, trans. Matthew J. O'Connell (Mahwah, N.J.: Paulist Press, 1988).

The Future of the Apostolic Imperative: At the Crossroads of World Evangelization

CARL E. BRAATEN

Introduction: The Crisis of Christian Mission

William Temple, the Archbishop of Canterbury, once called the emergence of Christianity as a worldwide reality "the great new fact of our time." In a similar vein a Dutch missiologist, Jansen Schoonhoven, called attention to a second "great new fact of our time," the ecumenical movement. World evangelization and ecumenism are two of the greatest achievements of twentieth-century Christianity. It was called "The Christian Century" — oddly the same century that experienced two world wars, the holocaust, and the gulags — and all of these horrible things happening in the heartland of Christendom.

At the beginning of the "Christian century," in 1900, John Mott wrote his classic, *The Evangelization of the World in This Generation*. The mood at the time was running high in terms of progress and expansion. Piety and politics joined hands in bringing Christ and Western culture to the "heathen" across the waters. An Ecumenical Missionary Conference was held in New York City in 1900. One of its leaders announced, "We are going into a century more full of hope, and promise, and opportunity than any period in the world's history."[1] At the open-

---

1. Quoted in Gerald H. Anderson, "American Protestants in Pursuit of Mission,"

ing of the conference President McKinley spoke of "the missionary effort which has wrought such wonderful triumphs for civilization."[2]

This was the time when Rudyard Kipling called upon Americans to "take up the white man's burden." The twentieth century opened with patriotic fever running high. America had just conquered the Philippines, an event that was heralded as a conquest for the nation and for Christ. Patriotism and evangelism went hand in hand. President McKinley spoke to a missionary delegation from the Methodist Church, and confessed:

> I walked the floor of the White House night after night until midnight; and I am not ashamed to tell you, gentlemen, that I went down on my knees and prayed Almighty God for light and guidance more than one night. And one night late it came to me this way . . . that there was nothing left for us to do but to take them all, and to educate the Filipinos, and uplift and civilize and Christianize them.[3]

By the end of the twentieth century the mood had changed dramatically. World missions, once the pride and joy of the mainline Protestant denominations, had virtually collapsed by the end of the century. Early in the century missiology had become a new theological discipline. In the seminary I attended — Luther Seminary in St. Paul — courses on missions were used to recruit men for the mission fields. Now missiology has become the orphan of the seminary curriculum. Meanwhile, the mainline churches have been shrinking by the millions, yet clinging desperately to their increasingly hollow identities. How can they even think about evangelizing the nations when they lack the nerve to evangelize at home? David Barrett, the author of the *World Christian Encyclopedia*, estimates that each week 53,000 persons in Europe and America are leaving their churches never to return.

The result is threefold: first, at the start of the third millennium the center of gravity of world Christianity has shifted to the third world; second, the Western nations have once again become mission fields, lands populated by neo-pagans, in the grasp of secularism,

---

Missiology: An Ecumenical Introduction, ed. F. J. Verstraelen, A. Camps, L. A. Hoedremaker, M. R. Spindler (Grand Rapids: Eerdmans, 1995), p. 384.

2. Anderson, "American Protestants in Pursuit of Mission," p. 384.

3. Anderson, "American Protestants in Pursuit of Mission," p. 381.

atheism, and nihilism; and third, at the same time millions who would still call themselves Christian are at best nominal church members, ill-grounded in the church's scriptures, creeds, moral teachings, and worship traditions. Where does that leave us? This lecture will be only the beginning of an answer to that question.

The Legacy of Christendom

The first part of an answer will call for all the churches to recognize that the age of Christendom is past, and that we must prepare for a future without its props, perquisites, and privileges. We will find resources for the Christian future after the death of Christendom only by going back to the sources of Christian origins and early developments prior to the Constantinian order. I believe we have yet to take the full measure of Søren Kierkegaard's prophetic "Attack Upon 'Christendom.'" Looking out upon Christian Denmark he observed that he could not find anything resembling the Christianity of the New Testament. Again and again he lamented: "Little by little Christianity has become exactly the opposite of what it was in the New Testament."[4]

Christendom originated in the fourth century when Emperor Constantine entitled Christianity to become the official religion of the Roman Empire and outlawed all its rivals. Christianity came to believe that it was the only religion with a right to exist, and didn't hesitate to use all means of coercion to enforce its beliefs. The church acquired an identity shaped by its symbiotic relation to political and military power and to social and cultural elites. The history is well documented and we cannot turn this into a history lesson. But we must realize that despite the Reformation and despite the Enlightenment the modern church, Protestant as well as Catholic, is in many ways an extension of the church of Christendom, still living off its legacy. Lutheranism became the state religion of the Nordic countries; almost everyone there gets baptized but only a few go to church. In Norway they are still debating whether any other religion besides the Lutheran should be taught in school. In Sweden they have just recently begun

---

4. Søren Kierkegaard, *Attack Upon 'Christendom,'* trans. Walter Lowrie (Boston: Beacon Press, 1956), p. 60.

to uncouple church and state. In the United States there is still a national debate about prayer in the public schools and the teaching of biblical creationism in science courses. Vestiges of Christendom survive.

Christendom brought about a massive distortion in two respects relevant to our theme. One has to do with the understanding of the relation between theology and mission, and the other between the church and mission. I am most keenly aware of the distortion brought about by separating theology and mission. Theology began in the early church as missionary theology. It was a fundamental expression of the apostolic church at work in spreading the gospel to Jews and Gentiles. The earliest beginnings of theology are rooted in the launching of the apostolic mission to the nations. Check it out with Paul, the first great missionary. All of his epistles were missionary tracts for the times. New Testament scholars today, whatever they think they may be doing for their own churches, would agree with the dictum of Martin Kähler, purely on the basis of the historical evidence, that "Mission is the mother of earliest Christian theology." Kähler said that theology began as "a companion of the Christian mission" and not as "a luxury of the world-dominating church."[5] Missionary engagement precedes theology, otherwise theology tends to become mostly an academic dialogue with current philosophies and ideologies.

The second distortion was the separation of church and mission. Once the tribes of Europe were conquered for Christ, they became part of the *corpus christianum,* part of Christendom. Entire populations entered the church by baptism; the state collected taxes from all its citizens to support the church and pay the salaries of its officials. The whole society was Christian by fiat, and the church became its chaplain. Officially there were no nonbelievers. The church was no longer a missionary church, in stark contrast to the apostolic nature of the early church. Mission was something carried on by mission agencies in faraway places. The church was something you found here at home; mission was something you did out there on foreign fields. Ecclesiology became static, not springing from the dynamics of the gospel on its way to the nations. Mission was a crusading activity of the churches aimed at pagans beyond the pale of Christendom. But

---

5. Quoted in David J. Bosch, *Transforming Mission* (Maryknoll, N.Y.: Orbis Books, 1991), p. 16.

the church was not thought of as essentially missionary, the instrument of a missionary God reclaiming the whole of creation as the realm of his rule. This static ecclesiology is reflected in official church statements. Take, for example, Article VII of the Augsburg Confession: there the church is defined as "the congregation of saints, in which the gospel is rightly taught and the sacraments are rightly administered." We are so used to hearing it, we think it is an adequate definition of the church. It is not. There is no reference here to the eschatological condition of the church's being and no reference to its missionary nature and purpose. Without linkage to the coming of God's kingdom and to the world for which Christ died, the church becomes turned in on itself — ecclesiocentric.

Ecclesiology with no eschatology or missiology is a legacy of the Christendom mentality that had to be corrected. The Second Vatican Council took a step in the right direction by defining the church as essentially missionary and mission as essentially ecclesial. A church without mission and a mission without the church are both contradictions. A missionary church and a missionary theology go hand in hand; anything less is a betrayal of the way the roots of church, mission, and theology are intertwined in the soil of early Christianity. In step with Vatican II is a useful slogan that came out of the World Council of Churches: "Mission from six continents to six continents." So we are seeing more Asian, African, and Latin American missionaries in North America and Europe. The notion that evangelism is what the church does at home to reclaim lapsed Christians and mission what it does overseas to make new Christians is a territorial distinction with no biblical basis. The evangel, the good news of the gospel, is the heart of the church's life and mission.

Re-Evangelizing in the Postmodern Situation

The idea that the so-called Christian nations of the West are as much a mission field as what lies across the seas has been slow in seeping into the consciousness of the churches emerging from the collapse of Christendom. There have been a few lone voices crying in the wilderness, calling upon the church to reclaim its missionary nature. In his Bampton Lectures in 1909 Canon Walter Hobhouse, after surveying the history of Christianity, charged that the church had become domesticated, had simply settled for a cozy niche, in short, had become a church without a mission to its surrounding world. He called upon the church to reclaim its apostolic charter, to be "a missionary church, not only in heathen lands and among races we are pleased to call 'inferior,' but in every country."[6] In a similar vein W. A. Visser 't Hooft wrote an article, "Evangelism in the Neo-Pagan Situation," in which he said: "It is high time that Christians recognize that they are confronted with a new paganism. . . . Christians have been very slow to recognize the pagan elements in modern culture. They were so convinced that the Western world was a Christianized world that they could not make themselves believe that pagan forces could exert a big influence in its midst. So they tried to console themselves by arguing that the new pagans were really Christians who expressed themselves in a somewhat different manner."[7] Then he goes on to say that the so-called Christian nations of the West have now become ripe for re-evangelization. A decade later John Paul II in *Lumen Vitae* called upon all Catholics to become engaged in re-evangelizing: "I urge you in the name of the Lord Jesus Christ, to make yourselves proclaimers of the gospel, to spread with all your might the saving Word."

Authentic evangelization must take into account the cultural situation in which the church finds itself. The church of Christendom became deeply immured in the culture of modernity. The nineteenth-century missionary movement was itself a religious expression of modern culture; in many respects it was a child of the Enlightenment. Too often the light in Enlightenment became confused with the light of the gospel. The missionary movement was an accompaniment of Western colonial expansionism. This brought the entire world within reach of the gospel. In the providence of God this was a good, yet ambiguous, thing. For the Christian belief in the uniqueness and universality of the gospel spilled over into the Enlightenment belief in the superiority of Western culture, the belief that its science and technology would deliver the pagan nations from superstition and ignorance. Gustav Warneck, a leading German missiologist, wrote: "It is certainly not by accident that it is the Christian nations which have become the

6. Wilbert R. Shenk, "The Culture of Modernity as a Missionary Challenge," *The Good News of the Kingdom,* ed. Charles Van Engen, Dean S. Gilliland, & Paul Pierson (Maryknoll, N.Y.: Orbis Books, 1993), p. 194.

7. W. A. Visser 't Hooft, "Evangelism in the Neo-Pagan Situation," *International Review of Mission* 65 (1976): 83.

bearers of culture and the leaders of world history."[8] Lesslie Newbigin, once a missionary in India, observed that one of the most popular missionary texts was the words of Jesus in John 10:10: "I came that they may have life, and have it abundantly," and, he commented, "'abundant life' was interpreted as the abundance of the good things that modern education, healing, and agriculture would provide for the deprived peoples of the world."[9]

It is easy to look back upon the modern missionary movement and see its faults, how it became a partner in trying to remake the entire world in the image of Western civilization. But my point is not to engage in prolonged analysis and criticism. The missionaries by and large did the best they could and were hugely successful in what they were about, planting churches and making converts, so much so that Christianity today worldwide is reaping the harvest they sowed. My point is rather to ask whether Western and American Christianity will fare any better in preaching the gospel under the conditions of present-day, post-Christian culture.

We have inherited a problem uniquely American, and that is the divorce between evangelization and church. The evangelistic enterprise has been carried by big-name evangelists — Finney, Moody, Graham, and the latter-day TV evangelists. Its overall effect has been reductionistic, individualistic, emotionalistic, revivalistic, and manipulative. Its engagement with the deeper issues of contemporary culture has been superficial. The established churches have meanwhile stood on the sidelines, keeping their distance. A second big problem is how to be authentically the church in a postmodern world. If the church of Christendom, and even its missionary movement, did not adequately succeed in critically transcending the limits of modernity, how will the church now relate to the culture of postmodernity without succumbing to its pitfalls?

Perhaps too much is being made of the difference between modernity and postmodernity. Some see a sharp discontinuity; others would rather view postmodernity as a way of accenting certain features that had been downplayed in modernity, with respect to knowledge, language, and metaphysics — just a reshuffling of the cards stacked against the church from its initial encounter with pagan culture. Some

---

8. David J. Bosch, *Transforming Mission*, p. 293.
9. Bosch, *Transforming Mission*, p. 293.

theologians are welcoming postmodernity as a relief from the bullying that theology endured at the hands of its modern critics. I am personally dubious that Christian theology will find postmodernism a more congenial ally. The fundamental issue is the status of truth. Whatever may be said about the modern missionary movement, the missionaries had no doubt that the gospel was true in the plain sense of that word. Postmodern thinkers are critical of two features of modern thought, what they call *foundationalism* in the theory of knowledge and *referentialism* in the philosophy of language. Modernism tried to build a house of knowledge on sure foundations. Postmodernism says there is no such sure starting point in giving an account of the things we hold to be true. In the modern concept of language it was thought that for a proposition to be true, it had to refer or correspond to an objective state of affairs outside the mind. Postmodern thinkers prefer an expressivist account of religious language. What you say is your take on things, your opinion, your interpretation, and it has no more claim on the truth than anyone else's. I think we ought to think twice before we jump from the frying pan of modernism into the fire of postmodernism.

Despite the postmodern attack on foundationalism, I still think of theology like a building constructed on the unshakable foundations of what God has given the church to think about. "The Church's one foundation is Jesus Christ, her Lord." That's a hymn Christians love to sing, and like unto it is another, "Built on a rock the church shall stand." Postmodernism, with its epistemological relativism, may not countenance such foundationalist talk, but Christian faith cannot live without it. And if language does not represent, correspond, or refer to an objective set of facts, then not a single statement of the Christian creed can be accepted as true. When Martin Luther ended his explanations of each of the three articles of the Apostles' Creed with the statement, "This is most certainly true," what he meant by "true" can be understood in the ordinary language of people in every age and every culture. In postmodernism we enter the swampland of religious pluralism and epistemological relativism, whereby one set of beliefs is as true as any other, and there is no way to adjudicate the difference.

The history of Christianity and its relation to culture should remind the church that its gospel will always retain a counter-cultural thrust that can never be accommodated, and that its truth claim can never be justified within the limits of unredeemed reason alone. No philosophy, ideology, religion, or culture can function as the sheath for the sword of the gospel. Each will need to suffer a radical internal transformation, under the judgment and power of the Christian truth. The long view of church history instructs us that the philosophers of postmodernism, whether Derrida, Foucault, Rorty, or others, are the new pagans whose spiritual ancestry reaches way back into the pre-Christian sources originating in Greece and Persia. The alternatives to Christian truth are not infinite. Forms of unbelief or disbelief reappear in every age, every culture. The history of the Christian mission first encountered Greek and Hellenistic culture, then Roman, Germanic, Nordic, Anglo-Saxon, Latin American, Asian, and African, and none of them has been an easy fit for the gospel. It is no different today in the postmodern, neo-pagan culture of Europe and America. Today the identification of Christianity with American culture has become excessive. We can expect a time of unraveling for the sake of gospel integrity. America, in all its cultural diversity, is our mission field, the place where we are all called to the task of evangelization.

Toward an Ecumenical Missiology

The task is too big for any of our denominations. Just as the modern ecumenical movement was born on the mission field, so now the new missionary situation in which the divided churches find themselves provides the occasion for renewed ecumenical commitment, one that takes mission as its motivating principle, in tune with Jesus' prayer that "all may be one, that the world might believe." Mission and ecumenism will together tear down the barriers of denominationalism, or the churches will retreat to playing the selfish game of competition.

The first imperative, then, for the churches is to work together to develop a new ecumenical missiology. And this is already happening. The three major blocs of thinking about mission and evangelization, once sharply distinguishable, are discovering common ground on what it means for "the whole church to bring the whole gospel to the whole world." Evangelicals, ecumenicals, and Catholics agree on that definition of holistic mission and evangelism as a starting point. Traditionally they met in different world assemblies, for example, Lausanne, Melbourne, Pattaya, and so forth, taking potshots at each other. Evangelicals would concentrate on spiritual concerns, saving souls, and eternal life, while ecumenicals would tend to speak of humanization, development, liberation, fighting against racism, poverty, and injustice. But more recently the language of the New Evangelicals manifests a wider vision. John Stott is a good example of the shift of emphasis. In his earlier writings he interpreted the Great Commission exclusively in terms of personal evangelism. After hearing the concerns of third world evangelicals he changed his mind: "I now see more clearly that not only the consequences of the commission but the actual commission itself must be understood to include social as well as evangelistic responsibility, unless we are to be guilty of distorting the words of Jesus."[10] But the evangelicals have not thrown the baby out with the bath. They still insist that the primary and essential task of the church is to carry the gospel across all cultural boundaries to persons who do not yet believe in Jesus Christ, to call them to faith in him as their personal Lord and Savior, and to membership in a Christian community.

Similarly there has been a struggle among ecumenicals to get their priorities straight. Evangelicals feared that the ecumenical churches were losing sight of the Great Commission, defining mission in purely horizontal terms, as liberation from oppression and poverty, as the quest for peace and justice, as lifting social and economic burdens. It seemed that evangelicals and ecumenicals inhabited radically different systems of doctrine, and this is plausibly still true if you compare the right wing among evangelicals to the left wing among ecumenicals. The left wing within the ecumenical churches are liberals who define salvation as liberation, replace gospel proclamation with interreligious dialogue, and substitute changing social structures for converting individual souls. However, there are enough evangelical voices among the ecumenical churches to pull the two sides closer together. The best ecumenical manifesto, entitled *Mission and Evangelism — An Ecumenical Affirmation,* exhibits the kind of evangelical focus and clarity that many evangelicals would accept. Its use of biblical, Christ-and-gospel–centered language would cheer the heart of most evangelicals. What we see going on is a remarkable new convergence. As ecumenicals have moved to embrace evangelical concerns, evangelicals are moving to accommodate ecumenical concerns. A good symbol

10. John Stott, *Christian Mission in the Modern World* (London: Falcon Press, 1975), p. 23.

of this converging trend was the appearance of Archbishop Carey of the Anglican Communion to address the Association of Evangelicals meeting this past summer in Amsterdam.

The convergence among Protestants has to a large extent been mediated by the strong role of the Roman Catholic Church in defining the mission of the gospel to the nations. Vatican II promulgated three significant statements bearing on missiology: *Lumen Gentium, Ad Gentes,* and *Nostra Aetate.* These were followed up by the Pope's encyclical *Redemptoris Missio,* and the most recent declaration published by the Congregation for the Doctrine of the Faith, *Dominus Iesus:* On the Unicity and Salvific Universality of Jesus Christ and the Church. Evangelicals have generally applauded the doctrinal contents of these documents, their view of God, Christ, humanity, sin, and salvation. They approve of their clear assertions that humanity needs salvation from sin, that God's revelation in Jesus Christ is definitive and complete, that Christ has commissioned his followers to disciple all peoples of the earth, that Christ is not merely one among many Saviors, and that other religions are not ways of salvation on a par with Christianity. Catholics and evangelicals have found a great deal of convergence in their understanding of mission and evangelism.

However, unofficial voices within the Catholic Church sometimes sing a different tune. Just as there are liberal Protestants who deny traditional Christian doctrine, so there are progressive Catholics who cross over the line. Hardly a particle of difference can be seen between Protestant liberals and Catholic modernists. At Maryknoll, New York (1981), some Catholic theologians were assembled to brainstorm on a "new missiology for the church." They were asked to outline a whole new approach to mission that could serve the church decades to come. They rejected as no longer adequate the traditional approach of trying to convert persons and to plant new churches. Christian proclamation is most effective, they said, when it takes the form of dialogue. Dialogue works better if we abandon the traditional belief in the universal need of salvation through Christ alone. The faiths of other peoples must be reverenced, and Christ is only a symbol of what God is doing in all the religions. Missionaries will henceforth be prepared to discover the seeds of the kingdom already growing on foreign soil; all they ask is to become partners in growing the kingdom among other peoples and cultures.

There is no future for an ecumenical missiology that would try to accommodate the heresies of Protestant liberals and so-called Catholic progressives. The Protestant John Hick and the Catholic Paul Knitter promote a new paradigm of Christian mission and call for a wider ecumenism that embraces all religions. All religions are equally valid, and their savior figures are as true as Jesus is for Christians. What they say is almost verbatim what Swami Vivekananda said at the World's Parliament of Religions a century ago: "Do I wish that the Christian would become a Hindu? God forbid. Do I wish that the Hindu or Buddhist would become Christian? God forbid. . . . The Christian is not to become a Hindu or a Buddhist, nor a Hindu or a Buddhist to become a Christian."[11] The spirit of relativism has taken control of the new paradigm of mission advocated by those who rush to embrace postmodernism. But there is nothing really new in it, since the philosophers of the Enlightenment, Lessing, Schopenhauer, Leibniz, and Herbert of Cherbury, as well as Troeltsch, Hocking, and Toynbee all taught that the reality to which the various religions refer is the same for all.

It is to the credit of the encyclical of John Paul II, *Ut Unum Sint,* that he places an ecumenical approach to evangelization on a track that can be embraced by ecumenical Protestants, evangelicals, and Catholics alike. Evangelization in Western culture, not to mention around the world, must go forward on a fully ecumenical basis, again that the world might believe and actually see that the love of God is not an empty phrase but has the power to work reconciliation between the separated churches. The encyclical asks: "How can we proclaim the gospel of reconciliation without at the same time being committed to working for reconciliation between Christians?"[12] In other words, how can the gospel be true if its promise to reconcile the world unto God does not visibly reconcile believing communities with one another? That is the scandal; that is the chief obstacle to effective evangelization, for which the churches are guilty. The Pope's encyclical asserts: "Believers in Christ . . . cannot remain divided. . . . How could they refuse to do everything possible . . . to overcome obstacles and prejudices which thwart the proclamation of the Gospel of salvation in the cross of Jesus, the one Redeemer of Man?"[13]

---

11. Bosch, *Transforming Mission,* p. 482.
12. *Ut Unum Sint* 98.
13. *Ut Unum Sint* 1, 2.

But ecumenical commitment to joint efforts at evangelization is not sufficient. Equally important is commitment to the full-orbed truth of the gospel and its creedal statements, without accommodating the isms of the age. Ideologies divide, and heresies give rise to schisms; only basic Christian orthodoxy — right teaching — has the power to unite and engender common endeavor among the churches. Here the encyclical is unrelenting: "The unity willed by God can be attained only by the adherence of all to the content of revealed faith in its entirety. In matters of faith, compromise is in contradiction with God who is Truth."[14] Here we circle back upon the issue of truth. Ecumenism and evangelization are like two horses that have to pull the whole load of divinely revealed truth.

Since Vatican II the churches have engaged in hundreds of bilateral and multilateral dialogues. Their aim has been to pursue the path leading to church unity. But they have reached a kind of dead end. The Lutheran bilateral dialogues with Roman Catholics have dealt with all the interecclesial topics handed down from centuries of mutual strife — nine rounds in all, engaging the best minds in both communities. At last we reached the signing of the Joint Declaration on the Doctrine of Justification in Augsburg one year ago. That was indeed an ecumenical breakthrough. But, I am sorry to say, all these dialogues and their final upshot have so far had minimal bearing on the burning issue of evangelizing in our post-Christendom era. The agenda of the dialogues recapitulated the history of past interchurch disputes rather than looking to the future of joint opportunity to proclaim the gospel that the world might believe. This note, "that the world might believe," the Pope's burden in *Ut Unum Sint,* has been virtually absent from the many rounds of dialogues between Lutherans and Catholics. And, I dare say, the same thing is true of the dialogues between Anglicans and Catholics, Orthodox and Catholics, Methodists and Catholics, and on down the line.

The ecumenical movement and its dialogues will shape the future of evangelization by bringing a wider diversity of images and points of emphasis coming from different ecclesial traditions. The result will be a richer and fuller theology for the long and difficult road ahead. Anglicans bring a theology of the Incarnation, Lutherans a theology of the Cross, Orthodoxy an Easter theology of the Resurrection, Calvin-

14. *Ut Unum Sint* 18.

ists a focus on the Ascension, charismatic churches see things in the light of Pentecost, and the adventist groups call our attention to the significance of the future Parousia. All of these salvation-historical events are essential in a complete christological narrative faithful to the church's Scripture, creeds, and liturgy, but when the unity of the church is shattered, theology also reflects the marks of division. Pressured to justify itself over against its competitors, each schismatic group tends to inflate the particular theological insight of its founder, reducing the whole history of Christ to a single category. Thus, for some of his followers Luther's theology of the cross tends to become the whole show. Evangelization in the context of ecumenism can serve to restore the integrity of theology as a whole, and to bring into play the fullness of the great theological tradition at the line of scrimmage where the church meets the world.

If that great theological tradition is brought into play, then the liturgy will be given its appropriate place in mission. Many churches in the evangelical tradition regard the church's liturgy as a liability in evangelistic outreach in today's culture. So also the sacramental spirituality of the church is treated as a hindrance. The light of the gospel that shines though the doxology and hymnody of the church is replaced by noisy gongs and clanging cymbals. For those who are seduced by the large numbers of people who flock to the shrines of McChurch Americana, we can only say, "Hang tough. Let's not sell our birthright for some homemade stew to satisfy our hunger for success and popularity." The worshiping community is a witnessing community, and part of its witness is letting people feast at the table of the historic tradition, which is far greater than anything we poor souls can cook up and serve on a Sunday morning.

Conclusion

We are certainly aware that the passion for evangelization can be rekindled only by the flame of the Holy Spirit. Theology can only be like the finger of John the Baptist, pointing in the right direction. We have said that the churches must together seize the ecumenical moment for authentic evangelization to occur. We have said that this ecumenical moment offers each community, each denomination, an occasion to transcend its own limits and to learn from others, in order to bring the fullness of the Great Ecclesial Tradition into play. Even the best theology in the world cannot perform the miracle needed to convert our enfeebled churches into agents of missionary obedience.

But theology can do what it is supposed to do for the church. Without retreating into a narrow orthodoxy, responsible theology faithful to the church must still draw some lines to exclude heresies and apostasies. The sad truth is that many of the theological best-sellers are filled with heresy. Theologies that do not work within the framework of the mystery of the Holy Trinity are anathema. Theologies that do not stem from the high Christology of the Nicene Creed are contrary to the Christian faith, and have no good news to tell. Theologies that break the special linkage between the kingdom of God and the church promote the secularization of Christianity, letting the world set the agenda. That yields the kind of culture-conforming Christianity that sent the church reeling in Nazi Germany, Eastern Communism, and now threatens the American church from the left and the right. Theologies that say that all religions are equally salvific, that Christ is not the one and only Savior of humankind, contradict the acts of the apostles, those first missionaries, and they deflate the entire missionary movement.

Those who believe that the missionary crisis in the church can be solved by new methods and techniques would be disappointed in reading nothing of the sort in this essay. Our supposition has been that what lies at the root of the problem is not methodology but theology — confusion about the message and the medium, the gospel and the church. The threat of postmodernity is the same as that of modernity — not how to communicate but what truth to communicate. In the days ahead the missionary encounter with Western post-Christian culture will get rough. The "powers and principalities," operating behind the backs of the dominant economic, political, social, and military institutions, will pit all their fury against the faithful who will not submit to their dominion, but choose instead the Lordship of Jesus and the way of the cross. The evangelizing church will at many points need to be counter-cultural, especially with respect to life-and-death issues confronting creatures and the creation.

The witness of the radical reformation has yet to be absorbed by the mainline churches. The majority of Americans are in favor of capital punishment and regard the advocates of nonviolence as extremists. In the future it will become clear that the disciples of Jesus, in an age of unparalleled violence, in our cities and between ethnic groups, will make peacemaking a fundamental part of their response to the good news of the gospel. Maybe it's time that modern Christians and churches, after centuries of taking sides in armed conflicts, in places like Bosnia, Croatia, and Kosovo, learn to curb the will to worldly power and simply heed the command of Jesus to turn the other cheek.

As we enter the third millennium we are still the people elected to bring the gospel and build the church in this post-Christian, post-modern, post-communist, post-denominational, post-whatever kind of situation in which we find ourselves. It seems that the gospel is too weak a message to persuade the skeptics, critics, and nihilists of postmodern culture. So we often try to dress it up in the latest styles to appeal to the cultured despisers of today. Theologians have tried to wed the biblical message to the thought systems of Hegel and Kant, Marx and Freud, Heidegger and Whitehead, and now maybe a few postmodern thinkers will be brought to the altar. The wonderful thing about the Christian truth, it has survived all these bad marriages. In a different connection G. K. Chesterton noted: "At least five times the faith has to all appearances gone to the dogs. In each of these five cases, it was the dog that died."

The missionary imperative will never change: to proclaim the mission of the triune God to the ends of the earth until the end of time. The Great Commission has never been repealed: "Go therefore and make disciples of all nations, baptizing them in the name of the Father and of the Son and of the Holy Spirit, and teaching them to obey everything that I have commanded you. And remember, I am with you always, to the end of the age."[15] The apostles and their successors have always mustered the energy, imagination, and shoe leather to answer Jesus' call to mission.

15. Matthew 28:19-20.

Contributors

Carl E. Braaten, Executive Director, Center for Catholic and Evangelical Theology; Co-editor of *Pro Ecclesia: A Journal of Catholic and Evangelical Theology*

Robert W. Jenson, Senior Scholar for Research, Center of Theological Inquiry, Princeton, New Jersey; Co-editor of *Pro Ecclesia: A Journal of Catholic and Evangelical Theology*

Todd E. Johnson, Assistant Professor, Institute of Pastoral Studies, Loyola University, Chicago, Illinois

John Milbank, Francis Ball Professor of Philosophical Theology, Department of Religious Studies, University of Virginia, Charlottesville, Virginia

R. R. Reno, Chairman, Department of Theology, Creighton University, Omaha, Nebraska

David L. Schindler, Professor of Fundamental Theology, John Paul II Institute for Studies on Marriage and Family, Washington, D.C.; Editor of *Communio: International Catholic Review*

Frank C. Senn, Pastor, Immanuel Lutheran Church, Evanston, Illinois

Philip W. Turner, former Dean of Berkeley Divinity School at Yale University, New Haven, Connecticut

Anthony Ugolnik, Professor of Ethics and Humanities, Franklin and Marshall College, Lancaster, Pennsylvania

parousia 24

SECULAR 7

MEN/WOMEN 16

HOMOSEXUAL CAPITALIST 17f

THE GOSPEL 79

CONVERSION 80

GRACE/LAW 11

ONE/MANY 108